What People are Saying a

"I am so grateful for my sister, Joanne, and her husband Ralph. They walk what they talk and live what they teach. Their passion to see followers of Christ walk in freedom and faith permeates every aspect of their ministry and every part of Victorious Living. As you study may you be stretched and equipped for God's glory and his Kingdom's increase."

- **Dr. James Bradford**, General Secretary
- Assemblies of God

"Victorious living is more than just an idea, it can actually be a way of life. Joanne Hoehne knows firsthand what it's like to be overwhelmed by life's challenges, but also how one can find answers to bring victory in the areas that once held you captive. In her latest book she gives us a step-by-step approach on how to use God's word to get on the other side of life's difficulties. Her sincerity and compassion are found in every chapter as she shares with us how victorious living was found by her and can be ours as well. This book will inspire you to live an utmost life."

-**Tim Storey**, Speaker, Author, Life Coach

"Victorious Living is not your typical spiritual study guide or book. It is a powerful, intensive curriculum that will strengthen, transform and restore the life of any believer no matter where you are in your walk with Christ. This is a must have tool for every believer."

- **Darryl & Tracy Strawberry** NY Mets & Yankees Baseball legend Founders of Strawberry Ministries and Clean, Sober & Saved Program

Victorious Living

The Life You Were Created To Live

JOANNE HOEHNE

Dedicated to my forever love, Ralph, and my sons Brett, Ashton, Connor & Logan that still amaze me every day. I am honored to be your wife and mother.

This book is our story. Thank you for not only sticking with me through it all, but most importantly for also stretching your faith and learning alongside me how to live by faith and trust our amazing heavenly Father to finish our beautiful story.

CONTENTS

FOREWORD
By Darryl & Tracy Strawberry

Victorious Living by Joanne Hoehne is not your typical spiritual study book. It is a powerful, intensive journey that will strengthen, transform and restore the life of any believer no matter where you are in your walk with Christ. Whether you are just recently saved, or have been a Christian for fifty years. This book reveals the truth of the Bible and leads you into the practical application you need to live the Christian life Victoriously.

Joanne is a powerful but practical teacher who speaks directly to the challenges the Christian believer faces in the world we live in today. Many Christians today are filled with information but lack the daily application that will lead them into victory. Victorious Living, through it's simple practical principles, leads you into an experience with Christ and creates a hunger within to live your life for Christ.

We have witnessed several powerful testimonies of people being freed from addictions and other bondages in their lives and even marriages, through the teaching in this book and curriculum.

This powerful book teaches the un-compromised truth of the Bible but illustrates the steps of how to live out that truth in our daily lives. Each chapter empowers and builds up the life of the believer one step at a time. This is the must have tool that will teach every believer how to walk out their salvation victoriously in Christ.

We see Victorious Living as a powerful tool for churches, small groups and individuals that will make disciples of God's people and lead them into Living their Victorious Life in Christ.

Darryl & Tracy Strawberry
NY Mets & Yankees Baseball legend
Founders of Strawberry Ministries and Clean, Sober & Saved Program

INTRODUCTION

God has such a sense of humor. He took a girl who was terrified of even leading a Bible study and turned her into a teacher and preacher. A girl who used to avoid writing at all costs, and told her to write books. But that's the power of God's amazing grace! He will often do things in our lives that normally we would totally be unable to accomplish on our own, and will leave us utterly speechless as He moves us toward victory. God has amazing things in store for all of us that are way outside of the boundaries of our own abilities.

Victorious Living is a book designed to help get us past our own limitations and lean into the amazing life God has for us. Many times we have all the pieces to a puzzle but do not know how to put them back together. Other times we find ourselves missing pieces, and are left unable to finish or make sense of the whole image. *Victorious living* is about finding those pieces so that you can see the whole picture of the life that God has planned for you. It breaks down biblical teachings into easy-to-understand principles that can be used and plugged into everyday life.

I have an amazing husband, Ralph, and four wonderful sons. This book was birthed out of our life experiences, the struggles we endured, and the victory we learned to walk in. God laid this message on our hearts in the fall of 2006, and we started teaching it side by side to a dozen people in our living room. God started doing miraculous things in people's lives, and we began to see the great importance of sharing the principles we learned with more people. Since then my husband Ralph and I have taught Victorious Living many times, which we have developed into a course. In 2012 we turned that course into a full DVD curriculum that offers over 18 hours of material.

The teaching and stories in this book belong to both Ralph and me. It is *our* story. It is our journey together in God that brought us through crises into God's Victorious Living. After years of learning how to overcome the setbacks that accompanied rough patches in our lives, and the revelations we learned, you can now take them with you. Through this book, I invite you to come on the journey with me so that you can also experience God's Victorious Living.

Joanne Hoehne
Co-Pastor of The Source Church
SHE Tour Founder

1

FOUNDATIONS

Have you ever felt hopeless? As if you were lost in the middle of a jungle with no clear pathway out? I have. My marriage almost didn't make it past its first anniversary. A few months in, it was already in shambles. We survived, only to run into more problems again a few years later. This time we had two young kids when our financial lives fell out from under us, borrowing money from our family just to put food on the table. In the middle of all that, one of our children was diagnosed with a life-threatening condition. It was horrible. I felt as if I were drowning with no way to reach the surface for air.

During that period of my life, I thought a lot about why things were going so wrong when they were supposed to be going right. Both my husband and I grew up in great churches and wonderful Christian homes. All our lives, we had heard that God was the great provider. That He was a Good God. So why wasn't He helping us when we needed Him the most? *"There must be a piece of the puzzle we are missing,"* I thought to myself. We were not seeing the "great plan" God had promised us for our lives.

In a search for answers, Ralph and I decided to attend a local church service. As the pastor began his sermon, I noticed that something was different about him. His message wasn't about religion; instead, he spoke about how to have a deep relationship with a God who wanted to be part of every area of our lives. His words moved us deeply. After he had finished speaking, the pastor gave an invitation to pray for whoever needed healing in their bodies. At first, Ralph was skeptical; having grown up believing that the "gifts" were not for the church today, healing ministries were nothing more than a scam. At the same time, Ralph also had arthritis in his knee and needed a miracle! So I nudged him by asking, *"what did he have to lose!"* After thinking for a second, he agreed and reluctantly made his way forward.

The Pastor laid hands on Ralph, and prayed for him. After the prayer was over and Ralph began to walk back to his seat, the Pastor said, *"God is also healing eyes."* By the time he sat down, Ralph had been touched by God. Not only was his knee instantly healed, something else happened that took us by surprise. From the time Ralph was three years old, he had to wear glasses to see clearly. After Ralph received prayer, he never had to wear glasses again.

Our encounter with God shook us to our very core. We both left the service that day asking ourselves, *"if we were lied to about healing, what else have we missed out on?"* That was the moment our journey to discover what God's promises were and how to access them began.

The words from the Pastor were the seeds of hope that began to change our entire outlook on life. After learning that God was indeed good, and had an incredible plan for us, we became forever grateful. We realized that the fault for our trouble didn't fall on God, but on our small understanding of who God is. We were excited for the future. Our newfound hope in God inspired us to dig deeper into what God had to say about our lives and the promises He has given us.

After 20 years of living with a new understanding of God and His promises, I can tell you that life is still amazing. The God who healed Ralph all those years ago is still the God who brings healing today. Through thick and thin, we have seen God's faithfulness and provision time and time again. It's that seed of hope that we now bring to you.

Solid Foundations

If you want to build a house that will last a lifetime, you have to build it on a strong foundation. Laying the groundwork is never the fun part of the building process, but it might be the most important. The same principle is also true in life. If you want to build a life that is strong and victorious, you have to pick the right foundation.

Two years ago we moved into a new home located on the outskirts of town. Our first home improvement project was to convert the oversized garage into living space. Our second project that we're currently working on is building a new garage. Due to the size of the garage we want, we decided to build a large steel frame building. The process has been lengthy, filled with dozens of delays and challenges. I remember after we had received the blueprints for our new garage, we were informed that we also needed an entire second set of blueprints from an engineer, just for the base of the building. You see, the foundation is so important that extra detail and attention often needs to go into it.

After having all blueprints and permits in hand, we were finally able to pour the concrete. We hired a professional concrete guy who came out, measured, framed, positioned bolts and necessary foundational stuff and poured according to our blueprints. When it was done, it all looked amazing, and we were so excited. Two years without a garage had become quite a challenge with all the stuff we have. Shortly after, it was finally time to install the frame of the garage. We were very shocked to find out that the measurements of the installed concrete were off by twelve inches from the original blueprint!!! The frame of the building was not going to line up with the foundation!! Even though the foundation looked great by itself, it wasn't until we started to assemble the building that we discovered the error.

The same thing can happen in our lives. We've all built our lives on a foundation, whether it was the right one or not. We may be serving God with all our heart, thinking that our foundation is the right one to lead us to live a successful life. It often isn't until we start to build our lives that we discover cracks. Disasters happen because somewhere along the way our foundation was built just a little bit off. That small gap grew into a vast chasm between the foundation we have and the foundation we should have.

As we go through this journey together, take the time to evaluate the foundation of your life, and whether or not you can make adjustments to line up your foundation with God's principles. When you build your life on the Rock, you'll be able to create a life that is full of power, victory, and joy. Redeveloping some of my foundational beliefs and fine-tuning others was the key to the victory in my personal story. It's amazing how such a little shift in a wrong belief or an almost-right belief to a truly God-based belief can make such a big difference.

Your Filter

The foundations we choose have a direct relationship to the way we see the world. It doesn't matter who you are, how much education you have, or what you've been through, everyone looks and sees the world only in "part." I am reminded of Paul in First Corinthians, *"now what I know is incomplete."* That's why when each of us comes to God, we often judge Him with preconceived notions of who He is and what He is like before we start our relationship with Him.

Having a preconceived notion is just like wearing sunglasses that are tinted green. It won't matter how much others try and convince you that the room you're in is white, as long as you're wearing those glasses the room will look to green to you. No amount of arguing or debating will change your perspective! That is why revelations are so powerful. The moment you realize the green sunglasses you're wearing can be taken off, is the moment you will see the truth others around you know. That God is much greater than anything you can imagine.

Most people will wear a lot of different pairs of sunglasses over the course of their lives. Even when a person can change these sunglasses, if they haven't had a revelation about what God says about His Children and His promises, those sunglasses will stay on. Our reasoning alone, no matter how valid it might seem, will not get us the victory we need.

Colossians 2:8 (NLT)
Don't let anyone capture you with empty philosophies and high-sounding nonsense that come from human thinking and from the spiritual powers of this world, rather than from Christ.

The moment the Holy Spirit shows us truth, everything changes. It's like the lights go on and someone is singing the hallelujah chorus! The fog in your life lifts and you can clearly see the Lord working. The confusion and lack of clarity that often accompany our struggles are exchanged for confidence and peace. We can see God for who He is and can fully grab the promises of God for ourselves. We then understand that it is only when we can view life through Christ, and the Word of God, that we fully live in all that God has for us. I pray that the Holy Spirit will start showing you *His* perspective for your life, and that we all start taking off the sunglasses in our lives that are holding us back from living shy of all God has for us.

God's Word is True

If you bought a brand new Mercedes, why would you flip through a manual for a Ford or Dodge to learn more about its features? Or would you rather read the manual written by Mercedes top engineers? The answer is obvious; you would want the manual from the car's manufacturer. They built the car, so it only seems right to assume they know the most about the car. Is the same not true when it comes to the Bible? If God is the one who created us, He should be the one we go to for the instructions we need to walk out our journey we call life. The Bible is God's instruction manual to us. He loves us so much and genuinely wants us to succeed. That is why He gave us a book full of promises, warnings, principles and spiritual insights.

The path to receiving revelations from God's Word starts when we accept that the Bible is inerrant; meaning without error or fault in all its teaching.

Numbers 23:19 (NLT)

God is not a man, so he does not lie; He is not human, so he does not change his mind.
Has he ever spoken and failed to act? Has he ever promised and not carried it through?

God has never spoken a word that was not true. He's never promised something that He isn't willing to fulfill. The Bible is God's written Word to us. Though so many have viewed it as a rule book of things not to do, the truth is far different. It's actually a book full of promises and principles that will help us live the most victorious life.

Romans 3:4 (NLT)

True, some of them were unfaithful; but just because they were unfaithful, does that mean God will be unfaithful? Of course not! Even if everyone else is a liar, God is true.

People, even pastors, and other Christians will sometimes hurt you or let you down, but God never will! God will always be faithful, and His Word will always be the same, yesterday, today, and forever. When we choose to build our lives on Him, we can rest assured we are standing on the strongest foundation of wisdom and truth in the universe.

God's Word, the Bible, is much more than just words on a page. It is a living, breathing text that, if followed, can bring mighty miracles into your life!

Hebrews 4:12 (NIV)

For the word of God is living and active. Sharper than any double-edged sword, it penetrates even to dividing soul and spirit, joints and marrow; it judges the thoughts and attitudes of the heart.

We pray that the word of God will come alive to you as you see what His word says about having victory in your life.

God is Good

Ralph, like many of you, grew up with the idea that if you don't do what God wants you to do, God's gonna get you! For him, the church was a place that literally scared the hell right out of you! There was a line that clearly marked where sin began, and if you crossed it, God would punish you. So as a teen, as many teens often do, Ralph walked all the way up to the line and started stepping over it. And, to his surprise, God didn't hit him with a lightning bolt! From then on Ralph concluded that it must have been a lie. The fact that nothing happened meant it did not matter if he crossed the line. He determined that if what he was told about God wasn't true, then maybe God wasn't as invested in his life as everyone said He was! Maybe God wasn't just a God that punishes, but also a God that wasn't really a part of day to day living! What Ralph didn't realize is that God is a good God. He's not waiting to 'get you' when you mess up. Instead, He's a God who is waiting with loving, open arms, wanting you to run to Him when you mess up so He can help you pick up the pieces and put them back together.

Jeremiah 29:11 (NLT)

"For I know the plans I have for you," says the Lord. "They are plans for good and not for disaster, to give you a future and a hope."

God has good plans for us! God didn't send Jesus to condemn the world, but to bring life to us! But we've bought into the lie that God is the one who is orchestrating the setbacks in our lives.

John 3:17 (TNIV)

For God did not send his Son into the world to condemn the world, but to save the world through him.

If you are a parent, I'm sure you have experienced this before. We have four boys. When they were younger, and one of them broke something, I can guarantee you that it was always the youngest brother that ended up taking the blame for it! He did not know how to defend himself and was an easy target for the others. Unfortunately, God has also taken the blame for many things that were not His doing.

God has given us over 7,000 promises in the Bible of great things for us. But we have limited our view of God to what we have experienced ourselves, heard from others, or by our simple lack of knowledge! We don't realize that God sent Jesus to save us in every area of our lives and allow us a way to access all His promises.

If we look at the Lord's Prayer, we see that God's plan is for us to live on earth, with the same blessings that are in heaven. Let me show you.

Luke 11:2 (NKJV) Lord's Prayer

So He said to them, "When you pray, say: Our Father in heaven, Hallowed be Your name. Your kingdom come. Your will be done On earth as it is in heaven."

Some of you may have never seen that before, but there it is! *On earth as it is in Heaven.* He does not want us to just "endure" this life until we get to heaven. No! God has a plan and purpose for us while we are here, and He wants us to experience a little taste of what heaven is like while we're at it.

The Benefits Package

If you were to go to work for a new company that told you they had a fantastic benefits package, wouldn't you want to know what all those benefits were? It would be crazy not to have access to medical care when you needed it, simply because you hadn't taken the time to read up on your benefits package! Or to get denied certain forms of care because you didn't know what treatments your health care plan covers. It's all too easy to find yourself at a disadvantage because you made decisions from an assumption. An assumption that could have been easily avoided if you had only taken the time to know what you were entitled to! What if it were all covered and you missed out?

Psalm 103:2-5 (TNIV)

Praise the LORD, my soul, and forget not all his benefits— who forgives all your sins and heals all your diseases, who redeems your life from the pit and crowns you with love and compassion, who satisfies your desires with good things so that your youth is renewed like the eagle's.

God provides a benefits package for us, even though many Christians aren't taking advantage of it. It's easy to think, *"I'm already a Christian. Why don't I see it already working in my life?"*

Hosea 4:6 (NIV)

My people are destroyed from lack of knowledge.

"My people" are those who are already serving God. We, as His children, are getting our butts kicked in the parking lot because we don't understand the program! So many of us are living far below the standard that God has for us, only because we don't know better. Believe me, what you don't know *can* hurt you. We need to find out what the benefits are that God has for us so that we can claim them and finally receive them.

Ephesians 5:17 (Amplified Bible)

Therefore do not be vague and thoughtless and foolish, but understand-ing and firmly grasping what the will of the Lord is.

God has called us to be intentional in learning and grasping the promises He has for us. To find out where our foundations might be needing a little adjusting. It's why He has given us a manual, the Bible. We need to search it and learn it; then we can access the benefits that God provides us through His promises.

2

OUR DOMINION & GOD'S KINGDOM

"Don't worry.... it will all work out!" Have you ever had someone say that to you? There's enough truth in that statement to be dangerous, but enough of a lie to hold us back from all God has. That statement implies that God can just come in and fix our problems purely because we have a need. If that were true, do you think God would allow there to be starving children around the world? Or that there would be random shootings and terrorist attacks? Or homelessness, abuse, poverty and addictions? Is that really the heart of our loving heavenly Father?

Let's look at His word.

> **Genesis 1:26 (NKJV)**
> *Then God said, "Let Us make man in Our image, according to Our likeness; let them have dominion over the fish of the sea, over the birds of the air, and over the cattle, over all the earth and over every creeping thing that creeps on the earth."*

"Let them have dominion." God took His rightful dominion over the earth, and chose to hand it over to man!

Can you believe that? Let me better illustrate. In an election year, we take President A, and vote in President B. Until the inauguration, President A has full control to rule as he sees fit. But once that power is handed over, President A no longer has any say! The power now fully lies with President B. No matter how much President A may see things going wrong, or how badly he wants President B to do something differently, he has no power to do anything about it. The only time he can step in is if President B goes to A and asks for advice or help. It's the same with God. Now that dominion has been handed over to humans, God cannot intervene unless we bring Him into a situation through prayer or operating with His authority.

Can you see how important prayer is? Or why we need to know who we are in Christ? Are you starting to see how God doesn't just act on His own accord to make our situation better? Sure, God can take any situation and turn it for our good. That being said, if you want God to act in your life, you first have to choose to get Him involved by using the authority He has given you.

The definition of dominion is *"the power to rule and control, to have final authority."* To have dominion means to be in a place of power. As the woman of my household, I have my own way of taking care of my kids, family, and house. As the man or woman of your home, you would probably say the same thing about your household! When you're in charge, you can decide how you want things done and when they should be done.

What if someone comes over and starts trying to change everything in your home around without permission? Without you asking, they rearrange your kitchen or the tools in the garage; they try to discipline your kids in front of you or give you unsolicited advice about how to manage your finances. It would be so annoying as well as out of line! Why? Because your house guest does not have dominion or authority in YOUR home. YOU do. Unless you give them permission, they have no right to change anything you do. As long as they are in your home, they have to submit to your authority structure, just as you would have to if you were in their home.

At the beginning of creation, God gave us everything we needed to rule and reign on this earth and be victorious. We were not created to be controlled or defined by our circumstance. Rather, we were designed to have authority, dominion, and power! The problem came when Adam and Eve sinned in the Garden. Their sin forced God to kick them out of the Garden and lose their God-given dominion. The devil took that dominion from them and became the ruler of the world. The good news is that Jesus Christ came and died so that we could regain the dominion that was rightfully ours.

1 Corinthians 15:21-22 (NIV)

For since death came through a man, the resurrection of the dead comes also through a man. For as in Adam all die, so in Christ all will be made alive.

Adam lost the dominion God gave him, but Jesus came to give it back to us. That's amazing news for us!

God's heart aches when He sees all the need and hurt in the world. But since dominion was handed over to us, He must sit and wait for us to take our rightful place as His children and do something about it. The problem is not that God ignores the cries of His children, rather, it's that His children don't know how to take their rightful place of dominion and authority, to be the change that the world so desperately needs.

When we submit our lives to Him and His will, we can inherit what Jesus took back from Satan and regain our dominion to rule and reign on this earth. That's why salvation through Jesus Christ alone is so vital to understand! When we understand we have authority; we no longer have to hope and plead with God to move in situations. We can start taking dominion and speaking to the mountains in our life and know they must obey.

Mark 11:22-24 (NLV)

Jesus said to them, "Have faith in God. For surely, I tell you, a person may say to this mountain, 'Move from here into the sea.' And if he does not doubt, but believes that what he says will be done, it will happen. Because of this, I say to you, whatever you ask for when you pray, have faith that you will receive it. Then you will get it."

Moving mountains is some pretty powerful authority. But here Jesus clearly tells us that He has given us that kind of authority, and we enact that authority through faith. When we believe, we are enabled to walk out our situation in power. When sickness is trying to take over your body, you don't have to plead with God to heal you, because the Bible says healing has already been provided for you.

Isaiah 53:5 (NIV)
But he was pierced for our transgressions,
he was crushed for our iniquities;
the punishment that brought us peace was on him,
And by His wounds we are healed.

So now we simply need to take our authority and command the sickness off our body in the name of Jesus. We cover the sickness with the Word of God until it wipes it out of existence. We let the *truth* of God's Word over-rule the *fact* of the circumstance. God has given us that kind of authority. All we need to do is understand who we are in Christ and start taking back our dominion in every area of our lives.

The Kingdom
There are two systems at work in the world today, God's system and the world's. Even though we can walk in the authority of God, we still live in a world dominated by Satan. It's only through Jesus Christ, and the fact He came as a man to take back man's rightful place of domin-ion, that we can operate with God's authority and in God's kingdom within the world.

I used to think that when the Bible talked about the Kingdom of God, or the kingdom of heaven, that it was referring to heaven. But scripture teaches us something different.

Luke 17:20-22 (AMP)

Asked by the Pharisees when the kingdom of God would come, He replied to them by saying, The kingdom of God does not come with signs to be observed or with visible display,   Nor will people say, Look! Here [it is]! or, See, [it is] there! For behold, the kingdom of God is within you [in your hearts] and among you [surrounding you].

The kingdom of God comes to us as we allow God's ways and thoughts to transform our hearts and lives. In this sense, it is not a place but a lifestyle of submission to God and His will. For God's Kingdom is God's way of doing things here on the earth!! It is in God's Kingdom where the blessings are. If we want to access His victory, we have to live in line with His Kingdom!

So just as God's Kingdom is actually God's way of doing things, the world's system is the world's way of doing things. Because Satan took the dominion over the earth away from Adam and Eve in the Garden, the dominion of this world and how it operates belongs to him now. By default, without having Christ, we live in the world system that is influenced by Satan and the natural tendencies of our sin nature that come from him. It is a situation we don't choose, but were born into. Learning to live in God's Kingdom is about stepping out of what are often our natural tendencies, and stepping into new God-given ways of doing things.

Matthew 6:31-33 (NLT)

"So don't worry about these things, saying, 'What will we eat? What will we drink? What will we wear?' These things dominate the thoughts of unbelievers, but your heavenly Father already knows all your needs. Seek the Kingdom of God above all else, and live righteously, and he will give you everything you need."

In every area of our lives, we have to learn what God's way of doing it is. It's not a one- stop shop where one revelation takes care of every part of your life! You may have had an Aunt Mildred who led hundreds of people to Jesus, but also lived in poverty and died young from cancer. At first glance, it's easy to see her good works and say she understood how God's Kingdom operates. If that were true, however, then why did she not see all of God's blessings in her life? The truth is, even though she had a profound understanding of salvation, she did not have a revelation of what God wanted for her health or finances. To put it a different way, she had a partial revelation. Even though she understood the revelation of salvation, she missed the revelation that, in the here and now, she could have lived out the blessings of God's kingdom.

We could easily substitute v. 33 of Matthew 6 with the phrase *"seek first God's way of doing things."* It would probably help us understand Kingdom better. As we seek to understand God's way of doing things we open up the door of provision for our life. God never purposefully withholds anything from us, but at the same time, He wants us to seek after Him and submit our lives to His will. In choosing His way of doing things, we show love, honor, and submission to him as The Lord of our lives. In response to us, He opens the door of provision of His Kingdom blessings.

As Americans, we are not naturally accustomed to the idea of Kingdom or kingship. We live in a democracy and know little about living under the rule of a king. Sometimes we forget that God's kingdom is not a democracy. We don't get to choose which spiritual laws we want to follow. Instead, we have to follow the laws that God gives us.

If you look at countries in other parts of the world that operate as Kingdoms, the royal family has ultimate power. The king does not need anyone's permission to do what he wants. He rules the country as he pleases. At the same time, he also bears full responsibility for the people in the kingdom. If anything goes wrong, there is only one person to point to. Even though he has ultimate power, he is responsible for meeting the needs of his people. Even though earthly monarchies don't do justice in explaining God's absolute rule in His Kingdom, they give us valuable insight into how God's Kingdom works.

Learning to live in line with Kingdom principles is not something you do overnight. It takes time to perfect. I like to compare building faith to exercising muscles in our body. Our bodies are made up of over 600 muscles. Each one is used for something different, and each one needs to be exercised and cared for a little differently than the others. Exercising your faith is like training for a marathon. If all you do is spend time building your arm strength before the big race, it won't help much! You have to train the right set of muscles for the journey ahead of you. We have to build all the muscles of our body to have total health. The same goes for our spiritual lives. We have to actively build all our spiritual muscles by learning the way God wants us to operate in *every* area of our lives. Too often we spend time developing one or two areas and end up ignoring all the other areas. If you are dealing with terminal cancer, this is not the time to be spending all your attention on exercising the spiritual muscle of finances. You need to learn to build all the spiritual muscles of your life while also knowing that each and every one needs a little different revelation than the other.

But it's not always easy, or everyone would do it!

Matthew 7:13-14 (NLT) The Narrow Gate
"You can enter God's Kingdom only through the narrow gate. The highway to hell is broad, and its gate is wide for the many who choose that way. But the gateway to life is very narrow and the road is difficult, and only a few ever find it."

It may be the narrow way, but God clearly shows us through His word how to get there. We have to choose it ourselves! Even though He is a sovereign God, He will never force something on you. Not even His blessings. Look at the choice He gives us.

Deuteronomy 30:19 (NLT)
"Today I have given you the choice between life and death, between blessings and curses. Now I call on heaven and earth to witness the choice you make. Oh, that you would choose life, so that you and your descendants might live!"

God gives us a choice. At the same time, He also lets us know what the outcome of our choices will be ahead of time. That's why He asks us to choose life over death! The choice between life and death can also be described as choosing God's Kingdom or the world's! We know that God's way will always bring life, and Satan's will always bring destruction. There are two systems, and in every area of our lives, we must choose which system we will be part of.

Love always starts with a choice. The fact that I chose to marry Ralph added a dimension of love that took us deeper than if I had been forced to marry him. It's the same with God. The fact that we choose God adds a whole deeper dimension to the relationship. That's why God gave us free will so that we could choose Him. Someone who has zero choices in their life would be considered a robot or a slave. God doesn't call us slaves but instead calls us sons and daughters.

In order to live in the Kingdom, we must choose it over the world. We can't have a foot in God's Kingdom and the world's system at the same time. In each area of our lives, we are either in or out of God's Kingdom. The choice is ours. We can either stay in our sin and way of doing things—which leaves us in the world's system—or choose repentance and obedience which puts us into God's Kingdom.

The Importance of Obedience

To put it simply, The Kingdom is accessed by obedience. It's vital that we learn to be obedient to what God speaks to us. While hearing the voice of God can be hard to discern, He has given us His written Word as our guide to hear Him. As we renew our minds with His Word, the Holy Spirit will begin to reveal what parts of our lives we need to change. To put it a different way, we will feel a tug on our heart to change a behavior or to start living differently. When this happens, it is different for everyone. But once you feel it, to willfully not respond is to walk in disobedience.

John 14:15 (NKJV)
"If you love Me, keep My commandments."

Have you ever been in a hospital and had to wear one of those awful gowns with the flap open in the back? The ones that leave you feeling totally exposed and embarrassed as you walk down the hall? Not the most comfortable or desirable experience. That's how walking with God can sometimes feel. It isn't always comfortable. Sometimes it feels as if we're out there with our backs exposed, completely vulnerable. Following God will not always automatically make you feel secure. Sometimes God will lead you out of your comfort zone to make room for what's coming next.

It's why Jesus said the path to His Kingdom is through a narrow gate. Obedience is not easy. It requires that we trust God enough to leave the outcome of our lives and choices in His hands. That we love Him enough to say we are confident in His character and His goodness. That's why Jesus says in John, *"If you love me."* If we, as His children, truly love Him, we must prove it by being obedient to His Word.

Proverbs 3:5-6 (NLT)

Trust in the Lord with all your heart; do not depend on your own understanding. Seek his will in all you do, and he will show you which path to take.

He's not going to leave you! When you step out of your comfort zone and obey Him, He will show you every step to take. And you'll start experiencing all the great things God has for you.

Isaiah 1:19 (NKJV)

If you are willing and obedient, You shall eat the good of the land.

Many times we are willing, but don't always remember that obedience must accompany the willingness. People sometimes think they can partially obey God and still walk in His best; or that they can pick and choose what commands to obey or not obey, and still be blessed. It doesn't work that way. Ninety-five percent obedience is not obedience. If you are required to run 20 miles to complete a marathon, running 19 miles is not enough. You can pat yourself on the back all you want for the miles you ran, but if you want to live in Victory, you have to be willing to complete the marathon. God needs us to trust Him by stepping out and investing 100% of our lives in Him.

Years ago God told Ralph and me to give an offering to our church over and above what we were already giving in our tithes and offerings. It was a significant financial commitment. He asked us to give $50,000 even though we didn't have it. When we heard this, we didn't know what to do! *"How were we supposed to give what we didn't even have?"* we thought to ourselves.

Even though we didn't know how to raise the money, we also knew that to get God's best in our lives, we were going to have to be obedient. For a while, we struggled. We even tried to negotiate with God. *"Maybe $25,000 would be enough,"* we said to each other.

In hindsight, we could have given a lesser amount, and the church would have been just as happy to receive a large donation. At the same time, God would not have been.

When we ask our kids to take out the trash, and they only take it to the door, are we pleased? No. We want our instructions to be followed to the letter. God is the same way. He doesn't want us falling back on our own understanding when things seem impossible. Rather, He wants us to trust in Him. So that's what we did. Even though we didn't have the full amount of money when we first heard from God, we committed to giving it as soon as we were able to collect it. After that initial commitment, God stepped in, in a big way. Over the next three months, God brought us all kinds of business. By the end, we had the $50,000 to give. So we gave it. That was the year our finances stepped out of ordinary and kicked into extraordinary. We've walked in financial victory ever since. Today, every time we hear from God to give a large offering, we give without hesitation. Let's be 100% invested in giving everything we can to accomplishing God's instructions, and let Him perfect the results.

It's A Personal Relationship

Many people know about God, but not nearly as many know Him personally. A personal relationship with someone is permission to spend one-on-one time with them. It's to have someone you can share your secrets with, and for them to share their secrets with you; to be there for each other and experience love between one another. That's what God wants with you. That goes way beyond just head knowledge or doctrine. It becomes close and personal. A relationship you can run to that is safe and intimate. God saves His secrets for those who are close to Him. As we draw closer to Him, He will share more of His secrets with us. What could be better than being let in on the secrets of the Creator, with someone who loves you intimately, just the way you are.

Romans 8:1 (NLT)
So now there is no condemnation for those who belong to Christ Jesus.

Anyone who has been around for awhile knows that we all mess up and fall short in life. People will sometimes forget that God understands this. He isn't sitting there with a big stick waiting to condemn you. Instead, God is patiently waiting for you to run into His loving arms and compassionate heart. When we mess up, all He requires is that we repent (to turn from our past behavior) and ask Him to forgive us. The power of the Cross is that, in Christ, when we fall, we can always start anew.

Learning the principles of Victorious Living is not about adding more rules between you and God. Rather, it's about learning God's way of doing things so that you can experience a personal relationship with Him. We are not earning His blessing or His love by following the "rules." Instead, we are getting rid of the barriers that hold us back from experiencing the fullness of God's blessings that He already has waiting for each and every one of us. He loves you unconditionally, and there is no way to earn that. Jesus is the only way to the Father. No amount of rules or principles can ever gain us that spot.

3

GRACE

Grace is a word that's synonymous with Christian living. It's also one of most misunderstood ideas in the church today. As a pastor, I hear people talk about God's gift of grace all the time, without having the first clue of how to use it in a way that can radically change their lives.

The Gift of Grace

Romans 3:24 (AMP)

[All] are justified and made upright and in right standing with God, freely and gratuitously by His grace (His unmerited favor and mercy), through the redemption which is [provided] in Christ Jesus

To have *Grace* is to have unearned, undeserved favor and spiritual blessing. I love that definition. Grace is unearned and undeserved. There is nothing you can do to earn it, aside from receiving it from God.   How awesome is that? Just like how a newborn baby does not have to earn the right to be part of your family. We don't have a list of requirements, standards and tasks that they must first achieve before they get to take your name and be part of your family. By their very birth they take claim to what is rightfully theirs; a place in your family. It's the same with grace. Being born into

God's family, through accepting Jesus as our Lord (or owner), means we can rightfully claim grace as ours.

When God first created man, He designed us to live in an ongoing personal and intimate relationship with Him. After Adam and Eve's sin separated Man from God, God's face became hidden from view. Human beings lost direct access to God's presence. In the Old Testament, talking to God was only something elite religious leaders, who were righteous enough to walk into the temple, could do. God's presence was reserved for a place called the Holy of Holies, behind a very thick, heavy veil that made sure God's presence was separated from men who were unclean. Priests had to go through extensive rituals to get ready for entering the Holy of Holies so they would not die while in God's presence. When Jesus died, that veil that separated us from the presence of God ripped wide open. The ripping of that veil signified that God was finally giving us access to His presence. The old way of having to go through a series of rituals to have access to His presence now was over. Through Christ, we can once again accept God's grace and directly connect to God in an intimate and personal way.

What does having God's grace in your life look like? Ralph and I have four sons that currently range in age from sixteen to twenty-four, three of them still live at home. They all know that, no matter their age, or where they may live, our house is their home. That includes everything in our home as well. Let me tell you, when they are hungry, they are *not* shy about taking all the food they want from the fridge. Why? They *know* that they have the right to be there. Yes, they always behave respectfully. That being said, our kids are never uncomfortable hanging out with us, talking to us, or asking for help. They honor and respect us and our authority, as well as the boundaries we have in our home, but within those boundaries, and in the environment of our home, they know they have love, protection, comfort and safety. They never have to fear coming home, or being able to talk to us about anything. They know they can bring their good, bad and ugly situations to us and we are there to help them navigate through it.

The same is now true with God. Through His Son, and the power of His grace, we can go directly to our Heavenly Father and spend time with

Him without fear or trepidation. We can talk to Him about our deepest joys, fears, needs and even mistakes with full confidence He is listening.

Have you ever messed up? I know I sure have. I am so grateful that God also provides forgiveness through grace. When we accept Jesus as Lord and Savior over our lives, His death pays the price for our sins. He not only forgives us but also lets us start over again. For some of us, that is the best news we've ever heard! Gaining a new identity in Christ frees us from having to live in the shadow of our past mistakes. As a pastor, one of the most beautiful things we get to see is how God can transform a life. Our church is a place where former addicts, prostitutes, and criminals can encounter God and find freedom. People struggling with depression and loneliness can find community, hope, and joy! After they meet God, they become new creations! They walk away from their encounter with God with their heads held high, ready to boldly witness to others about how Jesus changed their life.

God Draws You In

Ralph and I have been married for 26 years now. As much as Ralph likes to deny it, he pursued me for some time before I finally agreed to go out with him. On our first date, he bought me ice cream and took me on a walk through what would eventually be the neighborhood we bought our first home in. As we spent time together, there were so many things I learned about Ralph that I didn't know before. As we got to know each other, we discussed our dreams, what we wanted for our futures, and our faith in God. It was a night that changed my life forever. After hearing his heart, I knew he was the man I wanted to spend the rest of my life with.

Now imagine if that night would have gone differently. Instead of showing interest in me, Ralph spent the whole night telling me how lucky I was to be on a date with him. That he wanted a wife that would support his dreams and submit to his authority as 'the man'. Someone to cook and clean for him. To have his children and make him look good! Can you imagine? For a man to expect those things from a woman without having an existing relationship with her? Of course, I would refuse to ever go out again. For the men reading this book. I can tell you right now, don't even think about trying this! I can guarantee you; you will not get a second date. Why? Relationships are a two-way street. They are built on love and mutual respect, not fear and blind obedience.

If you listen to people, they often describe God in the same way I just described Ralph, as someone who comes to us with a list of rules and requirements a mile long, and only wants servants and subjects who follow His every word. In fact, nothing could be further from the truth! God wants us to serve him out of a relationship, not fear.

It's all too easy to fall into the trap of believing that God's grace is something we can earn. When we are in a relationship with Him, we don't have to live believing that if we don't measure up He will unjustly punish us. When our kids do something wrong, they still have confidence that they are our children. Just because they had a setback doesn't mean Ralph and I would disown them, force them to move out, and give up our last name. That's not how parenting works. They have a confidence in being part of the family that allows them to mess up, walk out the consequence, receive forgiveness and be totally restored again without ever being removed from our family. Why as God's children would we expect any less from our Heavenly Father? Grace gives us the confidence that we are firmly positioned in the family of God.

The bible says it's the goodness of God that leads a man to repentance. In the same way Ralph spent time romancing me on our first date, God want's to romance us to Him. To get to know Him, to trust Him, love Him and to desire Him. Eventually, after a successful romance, our desire to follow His Word will come out of a desire to please Him. Living a life of obeying Him is based in response to the relationship that we have developed, and not simply on a list of do's and don'ts. All of the things I listed previously about what Ralph could have listed as his wants in a relationship, eventually have indeed been things I have brought to him in our marriage. But it was not because it was a required list when we met, but instead, it came as a *result* of our relationship. Out of our love and respect for each other, I wanted to do those things.

Grace is God's romance package to us. We don't have to have it all together, nor do we have to understand it all at first. There's not a list of to-do's we have to fulfill. We often come to God, or we introduce someone to God and we expect them to understand and fulfill all the requirements of that relationship. We slam them in the face with all the rules and regulations. But they've had no time to get romanced by this amazing God! To get to know Him, to trust Him, love Him and to desire Him. The only requirement is to be willing to open ourselves up to Him. That's the beauty of having a relationship with God. If you are just willing to start, His grace will fill in the rest.

Resisting Temptation

When you actively choose to sin, you deliberately step out of the grace of God. A common but dangerous misconception many Christians have is that you don't have to give up your sinful pleasures when being a follower of Christ. That instead of living the way God wants us to live, grace covers it all!

> **Hebrews 10:26** (NLT)
> *Dear friends, if we deliberately continue sinning after we have received knowledge of the truth, there is no longer any sacrifice that will cover these sins.*

Scripture tells us that the wages of our sin is still death, even after we have accepted Christ. Infidelity is a perfect example of how sin can bring death to a person's life and relationships. They may be able to save the marriage, but I have yet to see a marriage that was not damaged by unfaithfulness. An affair can damage or completely destroy the healthiest of marriages.

The New Testament is full of stories that teach us about the power of repentance and the importance of leaving sin behind. That said, repentance is a process. Of course, no one gets it right all the time. However, when we do get it wrong, our response should always be to run to Jesus, ask Him for forgiveness, and make a conscious decision not to make the same mistake in the future.

Let's examine the story of the woman who was caught in adultery. When Jesus arrived on the scene He challenged her accusers by asking that the ones without sin should be the first to cast a stone at her.

John 8:9-11 (NLT) (emphasis mine)

They listened to Him, and then they began going out, conscience-stricken, one by one, from the oldest down to the last one of them, till Jesus was left alone, with the woman standing there before Him in the center of the court. When Jesus raised Himself up, He said to her, Woman, where are your accusers? Has no man condemned you? She answered, No one, Lord! And Jesus said, I do not condemn you either. Go on your way and **from now on sin no more.**

Jesus chose to show her grace, which excused her from the penalty of the sin she was guilty of. He willingly extended her that grace, but in return expected that she would turn from the sins of her past. That's how we should treat God's grace. To keep on sinning intentionally after God has freed and forgiven us is like spitting on the sacrifice Christ made to pay for that sin. Instead, treat your sin like a hot potato that will burn your hand if it's held too long. I had a friend once tell me this "Don't try sin, you might like it". There's truth in that! Often sin can feed our pleasures instead of feeding our spirit. The bottom line is, change your behavior. Decide to rule over it instead of letting it rule over you.

The Power of Grace

The little-known fact for many Christians is that grace is what will empower us to walk away from sin and live the life God has called us to. Not that long ago, I saw a statistic that said only 3% of Christians knew that God's grace offers us more than just forgiveness of sins. That grace is actually the power to live victorious and the power to help us live a life *free* of sin. The power of grace can make a difference in every part of our lives!

No wonder so many people are living defeated. They are not plugged into the power source! Living life without God's grace is like trying to toast a slice of bread without plugging in the toaster. Without electricity, the little button will just keep popping back up no many how many times you press it!

In how many areas of your life have you been powerless to change because you were not plugged into the power source? I'm here to tell you the good news that your days of being powerless are over. By grace, you will be able to do the things God has asked of you.

2 Peter 1:3 (NLT)

By his divine power, God has given us everything we need for living a godly life. We have received all of this by coming to know him, the one who called us to himself by means of his marvelous glory and excellence.

God want's to empower us! He didn't create us thinking we would follow His Will using our own strength alone. Through what Jesus did for us on the Cross, God showers us with all the grace and power we will ever need.

John 1:16-17 (AMP)

For out of His fullness (abundance) we have all received [all had a share and we were all supplied with] one grace after another and spiritual blessing upon spiritual blessing and even favor upon favor and gift [heaped] upon gift. For while the Law was given through Moses, grace (unearned, undeserved favor and spiritual blessing) and truth came through Jesus Christ.

God has heaped up blessings and abundance for us. It's not through the law, rules and regulations, but through His grace that we receive it.

2 Corinthians 9:8 (AMP)

And God is able to make all grace (every favor and earthly blessing) come to you in abundance, so that you may always and under all circumstances and whatever the need be self-sufficient [possessing enough to require no aid or support and furnished in abundance for every good work and charitable donation].

If you replace the word grace with power in 2 Corinthians, you'll gain a life changing revelation. At every new stage of your life, God will give you the power to do everything He wants you to do. He will not only empower you to be self-sufficient but will also give you enough to impact the people around you. For we are blessed to be a blessing to others. We were never designed to simply just get by. We were designed to reflect a gracious, powerful God.

2 Corinthians 12:9 (NLT)
"My grace is all you need. My power works best in weakness."

This is where it gets exciting! Through God's grace, the very things you are not able to do on your own, God will do through you. The more unable you are to accomplish the task in front of you, the more amazing it will be when God uses you to do big things! Grace allows me, a shy girl who never wanted to speak in front of even a dozen people, to be a preacher and teacher. A girl who hated even the thought of writing, to write books. There is no end to the possibilities of what God can do in and through you when you start to access the power of grace.

Accessing Grace
Imagine a big powerful rushing river with pristine blue water. You are standing on the shore, admiring its strength and beauty. The water is the clearest blue you've ever seen, so clean you could drink from it. That river is just like God's provision for your life. His grace (His unearned, unde-served favor and blessing). There is enough water in it to drink for the rest of your life. After walking up to the edge for a drink, you realize one sip will only quench your thirst for a little while. If you want to keep drinking from it, you'll have to build your house next to it.

You make the decision. After months of construction, your new home not only has a beautiful view of the river, it's close enough to reap all the river's benefits. There's just one problem! There is no way of getting run-ning water into your new home without proper plumbing that connects to the river. It doesn't matter how luxurious your faucets and taps are, without the necessary piping, you'll have to leave your house to get a drink. You can turn on every tap and faucet a thousand times, but without that pipeline, you'll never get water.

If the river is God's grace in this story, then the pipeline from the river to your home is faith. In life, you can do all the right things, but if you don't do them through faith, you won't get the results you want. To put it a different way, it's the faith that puts the super on your natural. It's the key that taps you into God's provision and power.

That's why so many Christians are frustrated! They are 'doing' all the right things but still can't access the blessings of God. They can even see all the promises God has for them, but they never seem to be able to access them. Their lives have become full of empty rituals. They are like the house with beautiful, luxurious facets but no running water. The key to accessing grace is faith. Therefore the way to access the answers to every need you have is faith.

4

FAITH

Hebrews 11:6
And without faith it is impossible to please God, because anyone who comes to him must believe that he exists and that he rewards those who earnestly seek him.

It's *"impossible to please God"* without faith. What an absolutely bold statement. But that's what the Word of God says. A life lived that is pleasing to God is a life lived by faith. That's why it's so important to learn what faith is. Many Christians believe "faith" is something that has only to do with personal salvation. It is indeed through our faith in Jesus that we are saved. That's one part of faith, but faith is so much more than that. In fact, it can be applied to every area of your life.

Many people pray, hoping God hears them and answers their needs. When their prayers go unanswered, they wonder why God answered someone else's prayers but not theirs. Some even start feeling there might not be a God, because they are crying out in desperate need and their prayers don't seem to be getting heard.

Understanding faith will transform the way you talk to God. Instead of *hoping* that God will hear your prayer, and being left to wonder why someone else got their miracle but you didn't, faith will be the lever that gets God's attention.

God doesn't answer prayers according to need, but according to faith. Just because you need something doesn't mean God will move miraculously in your life. We have to learn how to pray using faith so our prayers don't just hit open space. Instead, they'll go out and accomplish what you intended them to accomplish; strategically hitting the mark every time. That's what faith does. When you're operating in faith your prayer life will become incredibly effective. It will allow you to tap into the fullness of God's grace within your life.

What is Faith?

Exercising faith can be uncomfortable. It requires us to abandon our natural senses and rely on a force we can't see or touch.

2 Corinthians 5:7 *We live by faith, not by sight.*

2 Corinthians 5:7 explains this paradox. It represents the two systems in this world - God's Kingdom of faith, or the world's system of our natural senses. Even though we live within this world's system we have to choose to live like we're in God's kingdom. It sounds counterintuitive, but if we make life choices using only our senses, we leave no room for faith and will live a very limited life. The world tells us to *". . .believe it when I see it."* But faith tells us something different. *"I'll see it when I believe it."*

Read that again. It's the key that can unlock the power of faith in your life!

Ralph and I experienced this first-hand years ago, after God spoke to us about starting The Source Church in 2007. He told us that when we had a need, He wanted us to *first* step out in faith and *then* He would provide. Talk about a backwards way of addressing your needs! As business people, we had been trained to never ever move ahead on projects without a specific plan and funding. Now that we are choosing to follow God in a deeper way, God asked us to trust Him by moving forward even if we couldn't see how to plan or pay for what we were doing.

If God's ways were the natural tendency for us, every person in the world would be stumbling onto God's promises. Instead, God has given His children the secret pass code that enables them to inherit all His promises. That password is faith. But it requires trust.

You have to believe that God will come through on His promises *before* you'll see the benefits in your life!

Hebrews 11:1 (AMP)

NOW FAITH is the assurance (the confirmation, the title deed) of the things [we] hope for, being the proof of things [we] do not see and the conviction of their reality [faith perceiving as real fact what is not revealed to the senses].

Faith is something that happens *now*. Hope is for the future, but faith works *immediately*. Hoping for something is not the same thing as walking in faith. Hope is often our starting point. But it has to grow into faith. At some point, we have to make the transition from *hoping* something might happen, to believing that the promise is *already* ours and is *now* done, whether we see it or not.

An example of faith is a title deed, as Hebrews 11 states. If you have a deed to a car or a house, that car or house belongs to you! It's a fact, not simply a hope that you own it. That piece of paper is a powerful document that shows ownership. Whether or not you are standing in that house or sitting in that car at the time, the deed shows you have ownership. A title deed (faith) gives you ownership of a miracle!! Whether you can see it or not, faith says it's already yours and it's on the way.

Hebrews 11:1 (NLT)

Faith is the confidence that what we hope for will actually happen; it gives us assurance about things we cannot see.

Faith is the true confidence that what God has promised you will actually happen! When you have it, you can act boldly when you know the answer to your need is on the way. It's a confidence that says, no matter what your circumstance looks like, God has an answer, and He's going to show up at just the right time.

Faith & Belief

If you pick up a coin and look at it, you'll notice that it has two different sides, heads and tails. In order for a coin to be considered legal tender it has to have both of those sides fully intact. If the coin has two of the same sides, you won't be able to buy anything with it. It's useless.

The same idea is true for faith and its relationship to belief. Most people think they mean one and the same thing. Like two identical sides of the same coin. But they are not. They are two very different sides of the same coin, and both of them must be there in order to have access to what you are believing God for.

Let me ask you a question. How many of you believe that if you exercise every day and eat healthily you'll lose weight and get into shape? You'd probably say, "I definitely believe that." However, if I were to ask you as a follow up question, *"Knowing that, do you exercise every day and eat perfectly healthy?"* What would you say? I know I sure don't. Just because you believe you know how to get in shape doesn't automatically mean you'll take the steps to do it. That's the difference between belief and faith. Scripture says that even Satan and all his demons believe that God's Word is true. But they don't have faith! Belief by itself isn't enough.

Faith is the corresponding action that goes along with our belief system. The action we take that's based on what we believe. On the other side of that, without the belief that exercise and eating right will make you healthy, why in the world would you do it??!! To perform an action without a correlating belief that justifies the action is the definition of crazy. We need to believe and act in faith. In the Bible, there's a story about a woman with an issue of blood. Scripture says:

Matthew 9:20-22 (NLT)

"Just then a woman who had suffered for twelve years with constant bleeding came up behind him. She touched the fringe of his robe, for she thought, 'If I can just touch his robe, I will be healed.' Jesus turned around, and when he saw her he said, 'Daughter, be encouraged! Your faith has made you well.' And the woman was healed at that moment."

"If I can just touch His robe," she thought, *"I will be healed."* Even though she believed for a healing, she could've easily stayed home, hoping God would somehow heal her. Instead, she acted on her belief. She put her faith into action. Even though society had labeled her as unclean because of her sickness, and unable to be touched by others, she still grabbed the fringe of Christ's robe.

Jesus Himself acknowledged it was her faith that got her healed. Her belief drove her to radical action, past all obstacles. That action is faith. That's the proper balance of our legal tender of faith and belief, and it's what got her a miraculous result.

How Does Faith Work?

The best way to learn about how faith works is to read about how Jesus used faith.

Mark 11:12-14 (NLT)

As they were leaving Bethany, Jesus was hungry. He noticed a fig tree in full leaf a little way off, so he went over to see if he could find any figs. But there were only leaves because it was too early in the season for fruit. Then Jesus said to the tree, "May no one ever eat your fruit again!"

The following morning....

Mark 11:20-24 (NLV)

As they passed by the fig tree he had cursed, the disciples noticed it had withered from the roots up. Peter remembered what Jesus had said to the tree on the previous day and exclaimed, "Look, Rabbi! The fig tree you cursed has withered and died!" Then Jesus said to the disciples, "Have faith in God. I tell you the truth, you can say to this mountain, 'May you be lifted up and thrown into the sea,' and it will happen. But you must really believe it will happen and have no doubt in your heart. I tell you, you can pray for anything, and if you believe that you've received it, it will be yours."

When Jesus first cursed the fig tree, there was no initial sign it was dead. That didn't matter to Jesus. He knew it was dead, because He had cursed it. He didn't need to see it die. He already believed it was dead. The next morning, the disciples were shocked to find that the tree had died. Jesus, of course, was not! Why? He knew that His words went to the roots and that was enough. If the root died, the tree would die. Even if it wasn't right away.

Jesus tells us that, just as he cursed the fig tree, we can also tell the mountains in our lives to move. All we need to do is believe it will happen and have no doubt in our heart, and then act on it. Jesus spoke. That was His faith in action.

Did you also notice that Jesus said this was for "whosoever"? What He is saying is we can also do what He did. We don't have to have four years of Bible school or take a twelve week course to see a breakthrough. We don't have to have it all together, or know the ten commandments backwards and forwards! No. If we simply believe and act, we can operate in faith.

What's the mountain in your life that Jesus wants you to speak to, so it might move? Maybe it's your finances. A health issue. Your boss or your job. A marriage that's falling apart. A rebellious or hurting child. Whatever it is, Jesus said you should speak to it. We often spend way too much time speaking about our situation, and not enough time speaking to it. If you have a cancer diagnosis, speak to that cancer as Christ did to the fig tree, and kill it at its root.

For example, speak out loud: *"In Jesus name I curse this cancer and call it dead. Isaiah 53 says that by Jesus stripes I am healed. That promise is for me so I declare my body healthy and whole right now in Jesus' name. Thank you that I now walk in divine health and wholeness."*

Once you've spoken to your mountain, step number two is to walk away from it as if it were done. You may still have symptoms, and you may still have to go through a treatment plan with your doctor, but now you can have confidence that the mountain of cancer will be moved out of your life. You can start thanking Him and getting excited for the miracle to fully manifest. The world may think you're a little nuts, but let me tell you, when the medical report comes in saying you're "cancer-free," you'll be glad you dared to step out into some radical faith!

It Takes Time

We live in a microwave mentality society that's used to on-demand movies, instant meals, seamless communication through cell phones and emails, and five-minute drive- through windows. The idea that we have to wait for what we want is not an attractive idea.

I believe lots of people lose their miracle because they give up believing for it way too soon. One day, I think we'll all stand before God and He'll show us how close we were to so many things we had been praying for.

There is a great story about a man named Abram in the Bible. Even though he had no children, God promised Him that one day he would be a father of many nations; that his descendants would be as the numbers of stars. After God gave Abram his promise, it didn't happen right away.

Romans 4:18-21 (NLT)

Even when there was no reason for hope, Abraham kept hoping— believing that he would become the father of many nations. For God had said to him, "That's how many descendants you will have!" And Abraham's faith did not weaken, even though, at about 100 years of age, he figured his body was as good as dead—and so was Sarah's womb. Abraham never wavered in believing God's promise. In fact,

his faith grew stronger, and in this he brought glory to God. He was
fully convinced that God was able to do whatever He promised.

Wow.... I love that Abraham's faith actually grew stronger the longer he waited! I believe there are a lot of great things we can learn about God and ourselves during our waiting periods. Abram believed in God's promise so much, he changed his name to Abraham, which means father of many nations. That was his corresponding action of faith. Every time he heard his name, he was reminded of the promise that God gave to him. Abraham ended up waiting for twenty-five years before his promised son Isaac was born. The descendants of Isaac would eventually become the nation of Israel.

Sometimes it takes time for God's promises to come true, but don't lose faith while you wait! Years ago, Ralph and I had a son who was born with a life-threatening condition. He literally came within an inch of death more than once. For a long time, we put our faith to work, but didn't see a result. It took us a full year of believing before we saw him completely healed. Looking back, I am so glad that we didn't give up. Even though it took a year, I would rather spend the time applying my faith towards getting my miracle, than not and spend the next twenty years dealing with the disease. It's easy to feel discouraged while you wait. But believe me when I say your miracle is worth fighting for.

Someone On The Other Side

Years ago, before Ralph and I became pastors, God asked us to send our pastors on an all expense paid trip to Hawaii. At the time, we were doing very well financially, and just wanted to bless them for everything they had done for us. After we heard from God, we called them on the phone and told them what we wanted to do. After a long pause, they started crying on the phone. They explained that six years earlier they began believing God would send them to Hawaii, even though on a pastor's salary, they couldn't afford it. They were so humbled by our generous gift and how God had used us.

Initially, both Ralph and I patted ourselves on the back. We were feeling pretty good about ourselves until God spoke to our spirits. He told us, *"Do you really think you were my first choice? Do you think I wanted them waiting six years for their request?"* Once we heard this, we were immediately humbled and learned a valuable lesson. We were not the first people God told to bless our pastors with a trip. We were just the first ones who obeyed.

I truly believe there is usually someone waiting on the other side of your obedience! Every time you obey the Lord, you put in motion a miracle for someone else. As you sow that kind of obedience, God will in turn have others be the answer for the miracles you need.

Do I Even Have Enough Faith?

It's easy to read the story of Abraham and think you might not have enough faith to see God's promises manifest in your life. I can tell you from experience, it really doesn't take as much faith as you think.

Luke 17:6

He replied, "If you have faith as small as a mustard seed, you can say to this mulberry tree, 'Be uprooted and planted in the sea,' and it will obey you."

Do you know how small a mustard seed is? A few years ago we were teaching on faith at our church and attempted to hand out mustard seeds to everyone in the audience. Well, it looked comical to say the least. Mustard seeds are extremely small. But even the smallest seeds, when planted, can produce a large harvest. It doesn't take much. The same is true for faith. Even the smallest little bit of faith will kick your miracle into action. So if you don't have much faith, start with the little you have, no matter how small. All you have to do is plant it and watch it grow! I can show you how.

What Does Faith Really Look Like?

I could write a book about faith alone, what it looks like, and how it operates. Ralph and I spent years delving into the theology of faith, learning what it is and how it works. It took us a long time to work through it all before we figured out how to practically apply it. What we found was that once we discovered how to walk in faith, it wasn't nearly as complicated as we originally thought.

My favorite analogy to describe faith is to compare it to buying a television while watching the shopping channel. After you see a new TV you like, you call the number at the bottom of the screen. The sales associate asks you what size you want and what your credit card information is. After your order is complete, they say it will be delivered in 4 to 6 weeks. Now you're excited! You tell all your friends about your new purchase. You rearrange the furniture in your living room to accommodate your new television. As you wait, your friends come over and ask what you're doing! Even though you've told them that you've ordered a new television, they don't believe you. If they can't see it, they don't believe it.

I have a question for you. Just because your friends don't believe it, does it mean the television isn't on its way? Of course not! Can you still be confident that someday soon they'll see the proof?

That's what faith is like! Ordering the item is like our request to God for a miracle. His grace covers the cost of what we need. The delivery time is the time we wait for the miracle to manifest. The delivery is the actual manifestation of our miracle.

Now, as much as I love overnight delivery, sometimes it takes time to get our miracle. I don't know why some miracles happen fast and others take time. I just know that that's how it is! What I do know is that some of the most amazing journeys I've had with God have been during the waiting periods. For when you are waiting on God, you spend the time preparing for your miracle to arrive. Those acts of preparation are what we call faith! When you act as if it's going to arrive, speak as if it's going to arrive, and get excited that it's going to arrive! That's faith. Then, when it does finally arrive, you celebrate!

Unfortunately, just like the friends who doubted you about the television, people in your life will often doubt the miracle you're waiting for. They'll tell you that you're crazy for thinking it's coming. That you should accept "reality." It's in those moments, that your faith is grounded in a solid belief. If you aren't convinced God will perform your miracle it will be impossible to exercise the faith that He will.

Something that people often do is repeatedly ask for the same miracle over and over again. Instead of asking for it once, and spending the rest of their time exercising their faith towards it, they repeat the prayer and spend no time exercising their faith. To use the shopping channel analogy I just used, if the television you just ordered doesn't arrive right away (even though you were told there was a 4-6 week delivery time), would you pick up the phone and re-order the item? NO! Why would you purchase an item twice? We do that all the time in our faith life.

We say we believe God answers prayers, but then the next day we ask Him for the same thing again. We re-order our miracle. Then we get up the next day and re-order it again! If we are truly walking in faith, we would know that He heard our first prayer. From then on, we pray, asking, *"God, how do you want me to walk this out? How do I prepare myself? Give me wisdom while I wait."*

As I mentioned before, walking by faith is not the most comfortable way to live. Sometimes what you are believing God for is such a big miracle, it can feel as if you just jumped into a swimming pool with all your clothes on. It can be awkward and strange, like you're going to sink at any moment. Why? Because faith will always push you past your comfort zone. It will constantly stretch you to believe for more and to expect more. However, once you learn how to walk in faith, you'll get hooked on it. Like an adrenaline junkie, you won't be able to wait for your next dangerous adventure. You'll get excited when God asks you to step out in faith for the impossible, because you know that when your faith is in sixth gear, miracles do indeed happen.

Faith in Action

How do we receive faith?

Romans 10:17 (NKJV)
So then faith comes by hearing, and hearing by the word of God.

Faith comes from the Word of God! From hearing it. Whether it be by reading it ourselves or hearing it preached and talked about. Once we hear the word, the second step is to act on what it says.

Hebrews 4:2 (NIV) emphasis mine

For we also have had the gospel preached to us, just as they did; but the message they heard was of no value to them, because those who heard did not **combine it with faith***.*

We must be bold enough to apply what God's word teaches us, not just stop right after we hear or read about His promises. It's so easy to get excited, to hoot and holler, clap and "amen" when we hear someone preach about God's promises for our lives. But, it's not enough. If we want to see provision, we have to combine those promises with faith. That means we have to first believe in them, and then act like we will see them come to pass.

Two years after Ralph and I started our church, we were in desperate need of a new facility. In our prayer life, both of us felt God challenging us to believe Him for it. He told us not to fund raise, and to take one offering only. We virtually had no cash on hand. Let me tell you, as business people, we felt WAY out of our comfort zone.

God's request wouldn't have been that bad if all we had to do was hold on to the word God gave us and wait for Him to deliver a building. But that's not what He asked of us. He wanted us to act as if the building were already delivered. That meant actively looking for a building even though we didn't have the money.

The next year was a roller coaster ride. Eventually we ended up with a contract on a building. We still didn't have money or financing, but we had a contract. I'd be lying if I said Ralph and I weren't feeling the pressure. A few of our mentors questioned our decision. Church members started to wonder if we had taken this whole faith thing too far. We were being stretched. Regardless, we knew what God had told us. So we stood our ground. Then God showed up.

Three weeks before possession, two businessmen we knew stepped up, each on the same day, and told us that God had told them to give us the money. At the end of the journey, we walked into a church building fully paid for. His promise had come to pass, because we put action to our faith and held on for dear life.

To act in faith is to hold onto a promise and declare "I will NOT be denied!" Then live as if it's already taken care of.

Hebrews 10:38 (NCV)
"Those who are right with me will live by faith. But if they turn back with fear, I will not be pleased with them."

As true people of faith, we need to forge ahead, even if persecution comes or the miracle doesn't manifest in our time frame. Faith isn't the absence of fear, but the power to overcome it!

It's manifesting the revelation that God has given you—the promise or provision for your situation that He will bring the miracle you need.

5

INCREASING YOUR CAPACITY

"Why doesn't faith work for me?" I hear this question over and over again from people. It's usually because they don't yet totally understand how God's system of faith works. As it says in Hosea 4:6, God's people perish when they don't know the program!! When faith hasn't become real to them.

Years ago, Ralph served as a board member of the church we were attending at the time. One Sunday, our church had a special guest speaker who was from a nearby city. Before the service, the minister asked to meet with all the board members to discuss a few business-related issues. At the end of the meeting, the minister began talking to Ralph, asking him what he did for a living. Ralph explained he was in real estate and had been a real estate broker for over 20 years. Because real estate in our area had been slowing down at that time, the minister expressed to Ralph how sorry he was that he worked in an industry that was taking some hard hits. My husband explained that, even though things had been tough for others, it had actually been one of his best years yet. God had always helped him, even when the market was bad. God had always been faithful to show him how to think differently and be successful *in spite of* the market. Determined not to lose the point, the minister insisted that it must have been tough for Ralph. It couldn't possibly be true that Ralph had had one of his best years. That, even if things weren't terribly bad right now, eventually, Ralph would also feel the downturn just like everybody else. Again my husband responded by telling him He believed God was the source of provision. Still, the minister aggressively persisted, elevating the conversation into a heated debate. Not wanting to get into a fight, Ralph removed himself from the conversation and joined me in the main auditorium to be part of the service.

As the minister took the platform, he announced the title of his sermon to the audience: *How God can do the impossible.* About halfway through the service, I noticed that Ralph was pretty agitated. He even asked me if we could leave early. I couldn't figure out why Ralph was so upset. I thought the sermon was really good. All of his points were right on! It seemed to me to be an amazing sermon on faith and miracles. The difference for me was, I didn't know about the previous conversation Ralph and the minister had had.

On our way home, Ralph told me what had happened. As he shared, I instantly saw how frustrating the whole situation had made him feel, and understood his agitation. Judging from the sermon, it was clear that the minister had a lot of head knowledge about God and faith. What his conversation with Ralph revealed was that he didn't have a heart knowledge. Even though he knew the scriptures that told him God could do the impossible, he didn't know how to see the impossible happen in his own life. That's why he couldn't accept that God had provided miraculous provision in our lives.

Head knowledge alone is not enough to successfully live a life of faith. You have to also learn how to *apply* that head knowledge into your life as well. *That's* how you'll see your life change.

What's Limiting Us?

We can blame a lot of people, and a lot of things for why we are where we are in life. We may have no control over what has happened to us in the past, but in order to move forward, we have to take responsibility for where we are going. *We* are the ones who limit God by what *we* believe or think in our heart, since the word says He is able to do things even beyond what we could possibly imagine.

Ephesians 3:20 (AMP)

Now to Him Who, by the [action of His] power that is at work within us, is able to do superabundantly, far over and above all that we [dare] ask or think [infinitely beyond our highest prayers, desires, thoughts, hopes, or dreams].

So many people have told us over the years how "lucky" we are. I like this definition of luck: *"Luck is simply lots of planning, persistence and preparation."* A very successful friend of ours is constantly referred to as an overnight success. He told us that if that were true, it was the longest night of his life!! There's a lot of work behind every success story. The same is true about people with great faith. We need to deliberately chase after the great things God has for us, learn and chase after the promises of God, and prepare our lives for what God wants to bring us. *That* is so much better than luck, and belief is the place to start

Acts 16:31

They replied, "Believe in the Lord Jesus, and you will be saved—you and your household."

The moment we believe in Jesus is also the moment we receive the benefit of salvation. The same is true in every other area of our lives. We can be saved from sickness, from financial ruin, from hell, from failed relationships, and the list goes on and on. Our salvation starts, not when we received, but when we believed.

Our Capacity

I was born in Canada, not far from Niagara Falls. If you've never been to the falls before, it's truly a spectacular sight that attracts tourists from all over the world. The incredible amount of water that flows from the river and over the falls is nothing short of breathtaking. The interesting thing is that after all these years, the falls are still flowing just as strong, with no signs of drying up any time soon. Now imagine that those falls represent God's provision for your life. There's no limit, no chance of it running out. Even if every tourist took a little bit of water home with them, there would still be plenty of water to go around!

Now imagine there was a drought. The national park service tells you that you can take as much water from the falls as you need. There's no limit. The first person you see in line for water has a tiny communion cup with him. After they get the okay, they put their cup under the waterfall, and walk away with a communion-cup-size amount of water. The second person in line pulls out a gallon size container. After putting his container under the waterfall, he walks away with a gallon of water! The third person in line brought a large trash can, puts it under the waterfall, and fills it up. In each case, the size of the container determines the amount of water they are each able to take. The bigger the container, the more water they are able to take. Even when the water overflows the container, the size of the container still dictates how much water you can take away.

At this point the first guy is possibly a little frustrated. He got only a tiny little amount of water, while the final guy gets a huge trash can full! I can imagine the first guy saying things like, *"Who does he think he is? What right does he have to take all that water? That's just not fair! I want that much water, too."* I can imagine some jealousy and frustration rising up. But remember ... each person was given the same opportunity to take as much as they wanted. The only limitation each person had was the size of their container. No matter how much they wanted to take, their container size limited them.

The same principle is true with God. If His provision is like Niagara Falls, then the container we use is our belief system. Maybe, like the person with the little cup, you've been looking at someone else, wondering why they got a bigger blessing while you were struggling just to get by! Maybe you even felt that God favored someone else over you. I can tell you right now, no matter how much of God's provision you *want*, the thing limiting you is your belief. In order to take more of God's provision, you need to increase your capacity, or increase the size of your container.

If faith is the process of going to the waterfall, belief represents the size of our container. The more faith and belief you have, the more provision you can get. The more faith and belief play a role in your everyday life, the closer you'll get to having a permanent pipeline that brings you endless provision.

With the understanding that we can't extend our faith beyond our belief, or our container size, let me give you a real-life example. I repeatedly get asked questions such as this when we teach faith, *"So, you're saying I can pray for $1 million and I will get it?"* No. Not at all. My first question to them is: *"Do you have a bill that needs paying right now? Do you have the faith to believe that God will help you pay that bill?"* Often the answer is no. So my advice is to start with a container size of belief that you can handle. Why not believe God to bring you $50, or for a small bill to get paid. Then grow it so that a big bill will get paid. Then increase it so that you can get a pay raise, etc, etc. Eventually you will be able to increase your container 'til you get to the size that can handle a $1 million provision. Here's the key: Start where you're at, with what you can actually believe for. Grow from there. This is where many people fail in their faith. They are putting faith to things that are way beyond their belief level and wondering why it's not working. Don't despise small beginnings. There's no condemnation at all if your belief is still a small cup right now. It's simply a starting point. I guarantee that you can grow from there.

Increasing My Capacity

Ralph and I spent a lot of years doing life with a little communion cup. Let me tell you, it was not a lot of fun! Granted, we have also grown our capacity since then and have seen God do amazing things. Our goal is still to be hooked up to a permanent pipeline that constantly flows God's provision to us. We want our belief system to be at a place where we never put limitations on what we believe God can do.

So how do you increase your capacity? I'm so glad you asked. Here are a few things to ask yourself.

1. Who are you hanging out with?

> **Proverbs 27:17 (NLT)** *As iron sharpens iron, so a friend sharpens a friend*

We spent many years in an environment that was surrounded by friends who also believed for the miraculous, and we thrived. Our container grew massively. However, when we first moved to Florida, it was very hard to find other people or a home church that believed as we did.

At first we didn't think it would be that big a problem. *"We are strong in our faith,"* we told ourselves. *"We'll just walk by faith by ourselves."* After about a year and a half, we started to notice how much we were *not* operating at the same level of faith and provision that we had before. We realized that by *not* being around other people who believed as we did, our own faith had indirectly diminished. Our container size had gotten much, much smaller.

It didn't take long for us to renew our efforts to dig into faith again. We decided that—since we couldn't find people like us—we would take some people and train them to believe like us! That's how *Victorious Living* started. It was out of our desire to develop a community of people who could radically believe God for the impossible along with us.

Having people around you who can build your faith is a catalyst that can catapult you towards the amazing life God has for you. They can help you stay on track when you're having a bad day or encourage you to reach for new levels of belief and faith.

Having the wrong people around you will have the opposite effect. Instead of them rising to your level, often you'll just fall to theirs. If you're hanging around a group of people who all have problems in their marriage, it's only a matter time before you start to see problems in your own! Attitudes and belief systems are contagious. We have to be careful who we surround ourselves with.

2. What Are You Hearing?

> **Romans 10:17 (NIV)**
> *Consequently, faith comes from hearing the message, and the message is heard through the word of Christ.*

Note that Romans 10:17 does not say "faith comes by *having heard*?" It says by *hearing*. Hearing is current, present tense. It's ongoing. It's something that's happening right now.

There are two types of *hearing* that can grow our faith. The first type of hearing that can grow your faith comes from listening to people share their testimonies and stories. Hearing what God is doing in other people's lives can really encourage you and let you know that, what God has done for someone else, He can also do for you. At our church, every Sunday we share testimonies of what God is doing in people's lives, in order to encourage people. We know that the more our members hear about other people's victories, the more they'll receive the boost they need to keep believing God for their own miracle. It's a great faith builder.

The second type of hearing that grows our faith comes from hearing the word of God. God's word is living and active. As we listen to teachers preach God's word, it will build our faith! In our own lives, whenever we were struggling through something, Ralph and I would spend hours listening to sound teaching on whatever issue it was that we were dealing with. When we drove in our car we listened to CDs. When we watched television we watched sermons from our favorite preachers. It doesn't matter what you're going through. If you can fill your spirit with God's Word, it will encourage you and build you up!

3. What Are You Doing?

James 2:17 (Amplified Bible)
So also faith, if it does not have works (deeds and actions of obedience to back it up), by itself is destitute of power (inoperative, dead).

The more we learn how to obey what God asks of us, the more our capacity grows! God never starts us off with the really big tasks right off the bat. He lets us grow into it! That's why obeying the little requests are so important. If you're not obeying God on the small stuff, how can you expect Him to trust you with something big? I hear people ask God all the time for things like a prestigious ministry opportunity or a business deal that could take you to the next financial level. You won't be ready for the big until you've put in the time working on the little things He asks of you.

Luke 16:10 (NLT)
"If you are faithful in little things, you will be faithful in large ones. But if you are dishonest in little things, you won't be honest with greater responsibilities."

Statistics tell us that the majority of lottery winners go broke within three years of winning, regardless of the size of their prize. The reason: just because they've been given a large sum of money doesn't mean they're disciplined enough to manage it wisely. They haven't put the same amount of time in learning how to manage wealth as the millionaire down the street. He understands the true value of every dollar. A lottery winner doesn't. That's why most lose it all, and some even lose more than they've won.

The same is true within our journey with God. There are lessons and principles God wants to teach us along the way. Many of those lessons can be taught only through obedience. The little things in life that don't seem to have to do with our destiny or purpose, mean a lot to God. When you obey even the small stuff, and you don't understand it all, it shows God you trust Him enough to do what He says. God then knows He can trust *you* with more.

4. Am I Being Patient?

Hebrews 6:11-12 (NKJV)
And we desire that each one of you show the same diligence to the full assurance of hope until the end, that you do not become sluggish, but imitate those who through faith and patience inherit the promises.

If we allow it to, our trust and faith will *grow* while we wait for God to bring the promise. In hindsight, I can see how God's decision to let us wait for our miracle was the best thing for us. If we received an instant miracle every time we prayed over a sickness we wouldn't have pressed into God's word as much as we did. Waiting caused us to go deep. Today, we have a powerful healing ministry.

The waiting period is also a prime time for God to adjust your life, so you can be ready for the manifestation of your miracle. Don't despise his adjustments. God corrects you because He believes in you and wants you to walk into more than your circumstance. Yes, there might be a few unpleasant rebukes along the way. But it's worth it to let God refine and prepare you for the amazing plan He wants to accomplish through you.

The act of true faith is holding onto your promise and declaring "I will NOT be denied!!" Even if the process takes a little time, act as if it were done.

Putting It All Together

Philippians 4:6 (TNIV)
Do not be anxious about anything, but in every situation, by prayer and petition, with thanksgiving, present your requests to God.

All of this faith talk can seem pretty difficult to put into practice. We all have something we need from God! My goal is to get you to a place where you can be fully pregnant with the expectation of what you are believing for… Pregnant with your petition. One thing we have found very helpful is through Petition Forms–by taking this dense concept and making it tangible and practical.

We actually discovered this tool by accident! About 20 years ago Ralph and a couple of guys would meet for breakfast to study the Word and pray about what was going on in their lives. They realized, from one week to the next, they would forget what they had prayed about. So they started writing their requests down on paper. After, they would all lay hands on the paper and pray for those issues. What they discovered was amazing. The next week they found that many of the answers to those requests had come to pass! Miracles started breaking out week after week. Those three guys eventually turned into a group of hundreds who met every week. The more miracles they saw the more men they added to their numbers.

Does something magical happen when we write down what we need from God that couldn't happen otherwise? No. But I do believe that writing our need down, and praying in agreement together over it, enacts spiritual principles that unlock power into that situation.

Sometimes when we pray for God to move in a situation, the fact that God has heard us doesn't become real to us right away. It's easy to keep coming to Him with the same requests wondering if He heard us the first time. A Prayer Petition Form becomes a great tool to use as a way to *tangibly* hand over our issues and requests to God. When we combine the power of agreement in prayer over it God can do awesome things. If you start to worry about your situation over the days following your initial prayer, you can remind yourself that you wrote it down, and already handed it over to God through prayer. Now you can spend the rest of your prayer time thanking God for your miracle instead of re-asking him for it. You can pray for wisdom and direction of how to walk out the path God has laid to get you to that miracle. For God doesn't answer according to need, but according to faith. Later on, after God answers your prayer, you can add it to your growing list of miracles that God has done in your life!

All too often, we assume that God knows our needs! Sometimes we can actually forget to ask Him for the provision!

James 4:2 (NLT)
You don't have what you want because you don't ask God for it.

It seems so simple, yet how many times have we reached the end of our rope in a situation, only to *finally* realize we haven't prayed about it? When we do this, we indirectly make God our last resort! Instead of making God our last resort, this Petition Form helps us make Him our first resort. It helps us structure our need, and properly bring it before the Lord.

I have included a Petition Form in this book, so you, too, can start using it as a tool in your faith walk. We use these every week in our church, and every single week we see huge miracles come to pass because of it. It's the fastest way we know to walk people into faith, who may not have the full theological understanding of what faith is in its entirety. I hope you will use it! Better yet, share it with your small group or family. Have everyone write one out, then together pray over them and see how God moves!

You may think it's a strange thing to try, but I'd be a wealthy woman if I had a dollar for every time a person who waited months or years to write down their need finally gave it a shot and quickly got their miracle! One man had been praying for a reconciliation with his son for over two years, but had never written it down on a Petition Form. One Sunday he decided to try it. That very afternoon his son reached out to him asking for help! I've literally heard hundreds of stories just like that. Once again, it's not a magical solution, just a tangible way for you to enact the principle of faith.

I have to give you a couple of important disclaimers. Over the years we have heard a lot of crazy stories of what people have put on their Petition Forms. One man came to visit a couple of times when our church was a year old. He excitedly told us that the previous week he had written on his Petition Form that he wanted to have a sexual relationship with another guy's wife. He was so pumped that God was going to bring this all to fruition for him! Oops. Of course that is not the kind of prayer God answers. We quickly realized that there needed to be some clarification and teaching on some of the specifics of what we can put our faith towards.

The prayer of faith we talked about in Mark 11 can only be prayed when you *know* it's God's will for you to have it, or that it's God's will to move a certain way in your situation. We can never have effective faith if we are trying to apply it to things that are specifically against the will of God. We can believe for things such as healing, salvation for our family, and essential needs in our lives, as we know they are the will of God because His Word says so. But the job you take, the person you marry, etc., are just not quite so cut and dried. If you do not yet know what God's will is for a situation, then put on your petition that you are asking for direction and wisdom for those areas; that you are seeking Him and trusting that He will indeed lead and guide you into His perfect will for those areas. Let's be wise in this. I have seen too many people pray fervently for something they wanted, and God allowed them to have it. But when they finally did get it they realized it wasn't even close to God's best for them. Let's be wise and get into God's Word so we can correctly apply our faith.

My last disclaimer is this. Praying *"If it is Your will."* Sounds spiritual, right? But that little "disclaimer" people say at the end of their prayers is what kills more prayers of faith than I can imagine. Putting this in at the end of a prayer is more of a protection plan for us, I believe, than a real prayer. If God doesn't answer our prayer, we can only chalk it up to not being God's will! It takes the pressure off of our faith having to come through. That is far from the tenacious kind of faith that God wants us to have.

James 1:6-8 (NIRV)

But when you ask, you must believe. You must not doubt. People who doubt are like waves of the sea. The wind blows and tosses them around. A man like that shouldn't expect to receive anything from the Lord. He can't make up his mind.

"If it be Your will" is saying that you hope it's His will, but you're giving room to the fact that it may indeed *not* be His will. You're really not sure.

Jesus prayed *"If it is your will"* one time only, when He was facing the hardest experience anyone could ever possibly imagine. His crucifixion. His separation from God to carry the sins of the world onto Himself. He was desperate not to have to go through with it. He was looking for any chance that God would let Him off the hook! But when He got back into line with what God's will was to be, He went on to say *". . .but, nevertheless, not my will but Yours be done."* What He was doing was submitting Himself to God's will for His life. A prayer of submission. And we need to do that every day. Submit ourselves to God's will, and not only live a life that is filled with wanting to fulfill our own wants and desires. A life that truly seeks God's will for our lives. But that is the prayer of submission, not the prayer of faith. If you do not yet know what God's will is, then find out what God says about it before you start putting your faith to it! Get a Promise book and look up what God says about your particular need. Find scripture to back up what you're believing for. Spend time in prayer listening to His instruction. Make sure your want or need lines up with what God says. Then you will be ready to confidently come before the Lord in faith and speak to the mountain in your life, knowing you are in faith and that all doubt has been put aside.

The bottom line is that we don't know how God will choose to answer our prayers. Ralph always says, *"I don't care if God uses a dog to bring it in a brown paper bag, so long as He brings it."* The important thing to focus on is that God does indeed answer. We need to allow ourselves to get outside the box of imagining how we think God should answer it, and only trusting Him that He will answer in any way He chooses. It's that unexpected way of God answering us that keeps this faith walk oh, so exciting, as well as us being completely reliant on Him.

MY PETITION FORM

Why write petitions?
Philippians 4:6 says, "Don't be anxious about anything, but in everything, by prayer and **petition**, with thanksgiving, present your requests to God."

Writing a petition gives us a tangible, real way to hand over problems, worries, and situations to God. Our burdens and issues are now handed over to Him, and we give **HIM** permission to step in and work out the solution.

What do I ask for?
Habakkuk 2:2 instructs us to be specific in our requests to God. E.g., If you want a car, what kind do you want?

Write down **ANY** concern in your life. Examples could range from health and healing to financial issues or even relationships.

No issue is too big or too small for God. He cares about **EVERY** aspect of your life. If you need a job, He wants to bring one to you. If you need a date with your spouse, He wants to arrange things so that it will happen. If you have constant headaches, He wants to heal you.

The point is that He cares about **ALL** the details of your life and wants to answer them.

James 4:2 says, *"You do not have, because you do not ask God."* He just needs us to ask Him.

How do I pray over my petition?
In Matthew 18:19, Jesus states, *"Again I say to you, that if two of you agree on earth as touching anything that they may ask, it shall be done for them by My Father who is in heaven."*

Have someone pray over your petition with you. This is your time to ask Him to work out all your issues, and take the problems out of your hands.

Then thank Him in advance that He will do what you have asked. Faith is believing that we receive what we ask for, even if we don't see it right away.

After a petition is prayed over, continue to thank God in faith that what you have asked for is done (Philippians 4:6).

Date:_____

PRAYER PETITION FORM
HAB. 2:2, PHIL 4:6, MATTHEW 18:18

ASK GOD FOR: (First time requests only)

-
-
-
-
-
-
-

THANKING GOD FOR: (Things you have already asked for and are now believing for in faith)

-
-
-
-
-

6

YOUR WORDS HAVE POWER

"Sticks and stones may break your bones, but words will never hurt you." It doesn't take rocket science or much experience in life to know this old saying isn't true! Words have power. How many of us still feel the pain from words that were spoken over us when we were children? Or, how many of us still feel empowered because of encouraging words that someone said over us? Whether for better or worse, words do affect us, and therefore, they matter.

So, if words have such a powerful impact on us in the physical world, wouldn't it also mean that words have an impact in the spiritual world? That is correct! In fact, our very salvation is based on us speaking what we believe.

Romans 10:9
If you confess with your mouth that Jesus is Lord and believe in your heart that God raised Him from the dead, you will be saved.

We clearly see that the Spirit world is affected by what comes out of our mouth! Let's explore this thought further in Mark 11:23.

Mark 11:23 (NKJV) (emphasis mine)
*For assuredly, I **say** to you, whoever **says** to this mountain, 'Be removed and be cast into the sea,' and does not doubt in his heart, but*

*believes that those things he **says** will be done, he will have whatever*
*he **says**.*

I may have helped you out with the answer to this, but what is the key word in this verse? ***"Says."*** You got it. Jesus didn't say it *once. He repeatedly emphasized that, when we **"say"** or speak to a situation, it's then* that we receive it. Praying for it or hoping for it isn't enough! We need to speak to our situation. And speech requires words!

Proverbs 18:21 (CEV)
Words can bring death or life! Talk too much, and you will eat (have) everything you say.

Proverbs 18:21 (AMP)
Death and life are in the power of the tongue, and they who indulge in it shall eat the fruit of it [for death or life].

Wow. Every single word we speak chooses an outcome, death or life. The words we speak over our kids will either fill them with life or fill with them death. The words we speak over our finances brings life to them or death to them. The words we speak over our future will bring life to it or death to it. *"I didn't really mean what I said. It's just a figure of speech. It was just an emotional outburst."* Let me tell you something. There is no such thing as a neutral word. Words speak life or they speak death. Period. Proverbs 18:21 explains that we *will* have what we say. Not that we will have what we say, only if we really mean it. It doesn't work that way. What you say is what you will have.

Have you ever witnessed a person go through the very thing they predicted or constantly talked about? If you have, it's easy to think it's just a coincidence. I think it's something more! I've seen it happen a number of times in my life. I remember years ago, there was a beautiful young girl Ralph and I knew through mutual friends who always talked about dying young. Right before she became a teenager, she died in a tragic accident.

Her death was so sad. She was way too young to die. At her funeral, everyone talked about how she must have "known" that something like this would happen because she talked about it so much. As much as I believe that sometimes God allows people to glimpse into the future, I don't think it was the gift of foresight that made her talk the way she did. Rather, it was her words that formed her future. Tragically to a fatal end.

I remember another instance of a family who visited our church a few times. They had a young daughter who was deaf in one ear. Her eardrum had a large hole in it, and she hadn't been able to hear since it had developed a few years before. Ralph talked with the dad about healing and suggested they pray and believe God for a miracle. So they did. Ralph met with the family and prayed over the daughter. *Instantly* she was able to hear out of her ear.

The entire family was blown away! They had never seen anything like this before. There was no doubt something miraculous had happened. She could now hear perfectly!! After weeks had gone by, the girl's father was still struggling to accept what he and his family had witnessed.

When a miracle happens, you have to put logic aside and accept that God can do anything He desires. That was the very thing her father just couldn't do. Eventually, he took his daughter back to the doctor. After a careful examination, the doctor was amazed. He explained that the hole was still in the eardrum. From a medical standpoint, nothing had changed (I guess they forgot the little detail that she could *hear!*). The father agreed with the doctor and said, *"I guess she wasn't healed after all."* At that very moment she went deaf again. To the best of my knowledge, that little girl was never able to hear again.

It's a sad story. In the critical moment where it mattered most, the father chose to use words that brought death instead of life. Can you imagine instead if he had said something like, *"Well, I don't understand how, but I am so grateful she can hear with a hole in the eardrum! God is good!"* That would have brought life, and today she would still be able to hear. When you are met with a crisis, carefully choose the words you use to describe the situation. It could literally make the difference between experiencing life and death in your future!

It's very common that, when times get tough, we let our emotions get the best of us, and spout off whatever we *feel* like saying.

Controlling our Tongue

James 1:26 *If you claim to be religious but don't control your tongue, you are fooling yourself, and your religion is worthless.*

There's a great story in the Bible that demonstrates how powerful words are. In Luke 1, Zechariah, who was a high priest in the Temple in Jerusalem, prayed that he and his wife Elizabeth would one day have a child. After many years, and in old age, an angel appeared to him with news that his prayer had been answered. Even though Elizabeth was well past child-bearing years, she would have a son, and they would call him John. John would also not be just an ordinary child. He would grow up to be a great man in the eyes of the Lord as well as do great things. Look at the words Zachariah chose to respond with.

Luke 1:18 (NLT)
Zechariah said to the angel, "How can I be sure this will happen? I'm an old man now, and my wife is also well along in years."

Oh my goodness. *"How can I be sure this will happen?"* Really? Can you imagine? An angel comes down from heaven to talk to you. He tells you your prayers have been answered, explains how it's going to happen, and what God is going to do through you, and you're still wondering if it's for sure? It's nice when God gives you confirmation now and then, but most of us would interpret an angel showing up at our front door as a pretty good sign that God is taking our prayer request pretty seriously! Not Zechariah. He doubted the angel, because he couldn't wrap his head around it. On top of that, he *spoke* his doubt.

Luke 1:19-20 (NLT)
Then the angel said, "I am Gabriel! I stand in the very presence of God. It was he who sent me to bring you this good news! But now,

since you didn't believe what I said, you will be silent and unable to speak until the child is born. For my words will certainly be fulfilled at the proper time."

After the angel heard Zechariah's doubt, he turned him mute until the baby was born. Why did the angel turn Zechariah mute, you ask? Because the angel knew Zechariah would speak death to the miracle!! He would speak words of doubt and unbelief. God knew those words could kill the manifestation of the miracle. That's how powerful words are. Once the baby was born, Zechariah regained his speech and named him John. That same John would grow up to become John the Baptist.

Let's compare what happened to Zechariah with what happened to Elizabeth's cousin Mary in the end of the first chapter of Luke. The angel Gabriel also appears to her, telling her that she will give birth to the Messiah. Verse 29 shows us that she, too, was confused and disturbed by the message from the angel. The difference lies in their responses. Even though the message Gabriel delivered is even more unbelievable, she responds in a very different way.

Luke 1:38 (NLT)
Mary responded, "I am the Lord's servant. May everything you have said about me come true." And then the angel left her.

Zechariah chose death with his words, and Mary chose life. For as important a priest Zechariah was, he still didn't fully believe God could grant him this miracle. His words reflected his doubt. Mary, on the other hand, was shocked by the news. Even so, she used words that affirmed the faith in God she had in her heart.

You aren't truly *in* faith if your words don't line up with what you're believing for. You can't say you believe God will heal the cancer on you, if in the next breath you also make plans for your funeral. You can't believe God is going to take care of all your physical needs and then also say you'll never make it. That you'll never find the right job or have enough money. You'll only be in faith when your words line up with what you say you believe.

It was in reading Mark 11 we learned that we end up having whatever we say. Here is a list of common expressions that you might say all the time, but doubt you *want* to have in your life.

- *I just about died laughing!* (If you have to die, it's a good way to go, but do you really want to *die?*)
- *Oh, that kills me!!*
- *You poor thing.* (it declares poverty over that person…in case you didn't catch that one)
- *I am sick and tired.*
- *I'll never be able to…*

You get the idea. We often let words that denote lack and death creep into our everyday conversations. Satan is sneaky and often wins battles in this area because people just don't pay enough attention. *You will always have what you say.* Take it seriously!

Mark 11:23 (NKJV)
He will have whatever he says.

In Dr. Paul Yonggi Cho's book, *"4ᵗʰ Dimensional Living in a 3 Dimensional World,"* he cites a study that measured the effects of spoken words on water molecules. As scientists spoke positive words, the water molecules began to move faster and more energetically. When they spoke negative words, the water molecules slowed down and produced less energy. Considering that most of our body is made up of water, don't you think the words we use just might affect our bodily functions? Even science is proving the principles of God and how the power of life and death are in the tongue.

We had a woman in our church who had battled cancer for over 23 years. Every time she would beat it, it would come back again. What I loved about her was how positive she could be even in the midst of her set-backs. Yes, she would often describe how much having cancer "sucked," but in the same sentence she would also talk about how much she loved the different colored wigs she was now able to wear. It never seemed to matter how big the health challenges she faced were. Every time, she could find something positive to speak over herself. She used to declare over and over that the cancer wouldn't get her for long. That she was eventually going to win and live. Last year she went to be with Jesus, but not before living more than 20 years longer than any of her doctors thought she would. Her secret was simple. She chose her words. And they were words of life.

Psalm 34:12-13 (NLT)

Does anyone want to live a life that is long and prosperous?
Then keep your tongue from speaking evil, and your lips from telling
lies!

Your words will give permission to either Satan or God! I'll repeat that, because you really need to get this point into your spirit. Your words will give permission to Satan or God. No matter what situation you're in, watch how you react with your words. It matters!

Bless or Curse

Another way that words affect our lives is through blessings and curses. For words of life bring blessings, and negative words bring curses. Throughout the Bible, there are dozens of examples of blessings spoken over an individual, or a nation. Once that word was spoken it couldn't be reversed! The same is also true about curses. The Israelites understood the power of words. If we started looking at what we say from their perspective, we would probably be more careful about how we talk about our lives, our children, our marriage, our finances, and our future. I don't know about you, but I most definitely want to live under blessings instead of curses. It is through my words that I *choose* to live in that blessing.

It's an Overflow

We must discipline our mouths to choose life instead of negativity. I don't know about you, but sometimes, I think it would be easier to carry around a roll of duct tape just for taping my mouth shut on days I can't quite control what's on my mind! That of course, isn't the answer. The truth is that, even though we do need to control our mouths, our words are an overflow of what's in our hearts.

Luke 6:45 (NIRV)
"A good man says good things. These come from the good that is put away in his heart. An evil man says evil things. These come from the evil that is put away in his heart. Their mouths say everything that is in their hearts."

People are kind of like a tube of toothpaste. When they get squeezed, whatever's inside of them *will* come out. Have you ever muttered? Okay, so, maybe *you* don't mutter, but have you ever heard *anyone else* mutter? Is it ever positive? Wouldn't it be amazing if we could hear people muttering about how awesome they are, how great their future is going to be, or how blessed God has made them. That would be pretty cool! But no, muttering usually doesn't sound like that. Instead, usually a mutter restates the problem. *"How could they do that to me? I'm never going to get out of this mess. I can't believe they threw me under the bus like that. I can't stand that person. I'm sick and tired of all this. I wish they'd get hit by a truck!"* I think you get the point. Muttering doesn't usually bring life. But it's a pretty good indicator of what's in your heart.

Matthew 12:34 (NKJV)
For out of the abundance of the heart the mouth speaks.

Our words show where our hearts are. So, let's make sure we're speaking words that reflect what we believe and the direction we want to move in. For example, say you want to see a breakthrough in your finances. Your kids come to you and ask if you can take them to Disney World. If you don't have the money, a common answer you might use is *"Kids, We can't afford it."* "Can't afford' is a strong statement. It implies that things won't get better. Instead, say, *"Kids, We don't have the finances right now for that."* To say *"not right now,"* means that today you might not have the money, but tomorrow maybe you will! It leaves room for hope and expectation. It changes the way you look at the future. It's a subtle change in phrasing, but has a powerful impact.

Shifting your words can impact whether you see your future full of more of the same of what you've got now, or a future filled with miraculous provision and life. Trust me! You will mess up time and again with this. But that's okay. Just pick yourself up, ask God to forgive you for using negative words and get back on track again. This is a lifelong process. So don't give up! You can do it.

7

GOD WANTS YOU BLESSED

One of the biggest lies circulating in the church today is that God wants you poor, broke and humble. It's definitely an "interesting" way to interpret what a good and loving God wants for His children. Yet, somehow, we associate humility with lack. That's not how God sees it at all. Humility is what you call giving God the glory for everything! It's what you call not taking credit for the good things God does in your life. It's recognizing that, without God, you would have nothing. That's humility. And it has nothing to do with poverty.

When Ralph worked in real estate, he was the number one salesperson in his company for many, many years. Even though he made a lot of money, he always stayed humble. When people asked him why he was so successful, he *always* told people that his success was due to God's favor. He never took the credit away from God's grace and provision.

God needs us to reach our cities, communities and the world with the message of Jesus. How are we supposed to do that without money and resources? We can't. We have to break out of the mindset that says we should want only enough to meet our needs and step into the level of believing for *more*. We are blessed to be a blessing. God gives us provision so we can go and do the work of Jesus. He doesn't just bless us so we can fulfill our own desires. He blesses us so that *His desires* can be fulfilled.

I can tell you over and over that God wants you to prosper financially, but if God doesn't say it, it won't mean anything. What really matters is what God says. Let's find out what His Word says about financial prosperity.

Matthew 6:19-24 (AMP)

Do not gather and heap up and store up for yourselves treasures on earth, where moth and rust and worm consume and destroy, and where thieves break through and steal. But gather and heap up and store for yourselves treasures in heaven, where neither moth nor rust nor worm consume and destroy, and where thieves do not break through and steal; For where your treasure is, there will your heart be also. The eye is the lamp of the body. So if your eye is sound, your entire body will be full of light. But if your eye is unsound, your whole body will be full of darkness. If then the very light in you [your conscience] is darkened, how dense is that darkness! No one can serve two masters; for either he will hate the one and love the other, or he will stand by and be devoted to the one and despise and be against the other. You cannot serve God and mammon (deceitful riches, money, possessions, or whatever is trusted in).

Mammon is more than just money. It's the love of money, possessions and riches. It's trusting in money to answer your problems. The Gospel of Matthew is very clear, you can't love or serve God *and* money at the same time. What it does *not* say is that you can't *have* money. The question it asks of us is are you focusing your heart and devotion to God or to attaining wealth?

It's not easy to learn how to believe God for things when you have wealth. *Why would you need God for something when you can pay for it yourself? Why trust God for healing when you can hire the best physicians?* This is the logic of someone who has made money their source.

Some of the seasons in which I grew the most were seasons when I didn't have the available financial resources I needed. It *forced* us as a family to rely on God. For God's heart is that the wealth He gives us will be used to honor Him, not replace Him.

"Well, I don't know if God wants us to have money." Here's the problem with that argument:

Proverbs 13:22 (NLT)
Good people leave an inheritance to their grandchildren,
but the sinner's wealth passes to the godly.

How are we supposed to leave an inheritance for generations to come if we have nothing? God doesn't want our money to control *us*, rather, that *we* control our money. That's a big difference. In fact, it makes all the difference. When making money is our main motivation in life, every decision we make is about the bottom dollar. But when *we* control our money, it becomes a tool to accomplish God's purposes. We can have the confidence that God will continue to provide for us. And He can have the confidence in us that we serve Him, not the almighty dollar.

Jesus spent a great deal of time during his ministry talking about money. When people asked Him why he came to earth, He would often say:

Luke 4:18 (NLT)
"The Spirit of the Lord is upon me, for he has anointed me to bring
Good News to the poor."

The first thing Jesus said was that He was here to bring good news to the poor. What is good news to a poor person? That you have to stay poor for the rest of your life? That Jesus loves you but you've got to suck it up 'til you get to heaven? No! It's that you don't have to be poor anymore.

I want to be clear here. Over the last few decades, a number of well-known ministers have preached a prosperity gospel. Some have taught the message, that God blesses His children, in an unhealthy way. How many of you know that for every mile of road, there's two miles of ditch? To put it differently, for every piece of truth, there's two possible extremes. The prosperity Gospel is one of those extremes. On one side, you have Christians who argue that having money is bad. As people of faith, we should stay poor. On the other, there are preachers who say all you need to do is "name it and claim it." That if you believe God for the desires of your heart, you can have it. That we can all be millionaires! That God's blessings have nothing to do with helping us fulfill God's plan for our lives, and everything to do with fulfilling our own desires.

I believe there is balance in the middle. Our definition of prosperity comes from the following scripture.

2 Corinthians 9:8 (AMP)

And God is able to make all grace (every favor and earthly blessing) come to you in abundance, so that you may always and under all circumstances and whatever the need be self-sufficient [possessing enough to require no aid or support and furnished in abundance for every good work and charitable donation].

We believe that prosperity is having all your needs met, and enough left over to do everything that God has called you to do. This means that prosperity looks different for every person! If someone is called to be a prayer warrior, spending 12 hours a day on their knees praying for the church, they don't need the same wealth as someone in the business world, who has been called to donate millions to build churches and expand ministries! The calling on our lives will determine what prosperity looks like for each of us.

Deuteronomy 8:18 (NKJV)

And you shall remember the Lord your God, for it is He who gives you power to get wealth, that He may establish His covenant which He swore to your fathers, as it is this day.

I love that this verse says it's God who gives us the ability to create wealth. This should keep us humble, but it should also give us hope! As we allow God to come into our finances, He can give us abilities we would have never otherwise had.

Deuteronomy also tells us the reason God gives us wealth, and that is to establish His covenant. In other words, to fulfill a promise God gave us through Abraham. That we would be blessed, and through that blessing the world would be drawn back to God. There is so much more at stake when it comes to finances, than just our own comfort.

Though God's ultimate goal with finances is to grow His Kingdom, He also provides lavishly for us in the process. He is clearly not a *"just barely getting by"* kind of God. Look at how He wants to provide for our needs.

Matthew 6:25-33 (Amp)

Therefore I tell you, stop being perpetually uneasy (anxious and worried) about your life, what you shall eat or what you shall drink; or about your body, what you shall put on. Is not life greater [in quality] than food, and the body [far above and more excellent] than clothing? Look at the birds of the air; they neither sow nor reap nor gather into barns, and yet your heavenly Father keeps feeding them. Are you not worth much more than they? And who of you by worrying and being anxious can add one unit of measure (cubit) to his stature or to the span of his life? And why should you be anxious about clothes? Consider the lilies of the field and learn thoroughly how they grow; they neither toil nor spin. Yet I tell you, even Solomon in all his magnificence (excellence, dignity, and grace) was not arrayed like one of these. [I Kings 10:4-7.] But if God so clothes the grass of the field, which today is alive and green and tomorrow is tossed into the furnace, will He not much more surely clothe you, O you of little faith? Therefore do not worry and be anxious, saying, What are we going to have to eat? or, What are we going to have to drink? or, What are we going to have to wear? For the Gentiles (heathens) wish for and crave and diligently seek all these things, and your heavenly Father knows well that you need them all. But seek (aim at and strive after) first of all His kingdom and His righteousness (His way of doing and being right), and then all these things taken together will be given you besides.

What amazing provision! The key to accessing it is located in the final part of that passage. We have to seek *His* way of doing things. We have to step into His kingdom principles. We can't pray for provision, and insist on doing it our own way. When it comes to finances, we have to find out what He says first, and then obey it! The story of Peter fishing explains this perfectly.

Luke 5:1-9 (NKJV)

So it was, as the multitude pressed about Him to hear the word of God, that He stood by the Lake of Gennesaret, and saw two boats standing by the lake; but the fishermen had gone from them and were washing their nets. Then He got into one of the boats, which was Simon's, and asked him to put out a little from the land. And He sat down and taught the multitudes from the boat. When He had stopped speaking, He said to Simon, "Launch out into the deep and let down your nets for a catch." But Simon answered and said to Him, "Master, we have toiled all night and caught nothing; nevertheless at Your word I will let down the net." And when they had done this, they caught a great number of fish, and their net was breaking. So they signaled to their partners in the other boat to come and help them. And they came and filled both the boats, so that they began to sink. When Simon Peter saw it, he fell down at Jesus' knees, saying, "Depart from me, for I am a sinful man, O Lord!" For he and all who were with him were astonished at the catch of fish which they had taken here.

Simon Peter had to go against every bit of common sense to do what Jesus was asking. Jesus told him to put down his nets even after he had fished unsuccessfully all night. Peter was a professional fisherman. He knew what Jesus was asking was crazy! It made no sense. But he obeyed regardless. Notice that Peter only partially obeyed. That's why he asked for forgiveness at the end of the story. For he had doubted Jesus and did the least. But even so, Jesus still brought overwhelming provision! Can you imagine how many fish Peter would have caught had he cast all his nets as Jesus had originally asked for? Our level of obedience, despite what our natural brain can comprehend, determines the level of blessing that can be released to us.

Who's Your Source?

Ralph and I celebrated our 26th Wedding Anniversary this year. The joke in our family is that I married him for his money! My kids love to pull this one out and harass me with it. Though, of course, it's not the reason I married him, there IS a grain of truth in it. Let me explain myself before you rush to conclusions.

When I first met Ralph it was obvious he was successful. At only twenty three years of age, he already drove a nice Mercedes, owned several homes, as well as a real estate company that had over 20 employees working under him. My impression of him was that he was confident, the kind of guy who seemed to get whatever he wanted. The only problem was, I wasn't interested! Even though he seemed nice, he wasn't my typical "type" of guy. Still, after a LOT of asking, I finally agreed to let Ralph take me out for ice cream. *"He's a successful guy who drives a nice car,"* I told myself, *"There are worse ways to spend an evening."*

Even though my initial reasons for going out with Ralph were shallow, little did I know I would discover an amazing man who, after getting to know him, was the person I knew I would be with forever. It's true, I didn't marry Ralph for his money. But I did marry him for the many character traits and qualities that *did* make him wealthy and successful. He was a man who knew what he wanted. When he went after something, he would usually get it! He had a strong work ethic and was a creative thinker. He was great with people and full of integrity.

Shortly after, we got married and rode his success for a long time. Then one day, the success was over. We hit a rough patch. The doors that were once open had closed. Five years into our marriage we were totally broke, borrowing money for food. Our lives were 180 degrees different than just a few years earlier.

I remember, both Ralph and I went through a crisis of faith. For years we had done everything right. We went to church, read the word, and regularly tithed. If God loved us so much, and wanted us to prosper, why were we in this mess? That's when God gave us a revelation of a lifetime. Even though we were obedient to God, we had still put all our trust in Ralph's ability to make provision for our lives, and not in God's.

Looking back, I'm so glad God let us go through a desert experience. If it weren't for the struggle, we would never have learned what it meant to fully trust in Him. From that day forward, we made a decision as a family that God *had* to be our source. Our abilities were just the tools that God used to bless us, but they were *not* our source. Only God could be trusted to care for us.

The Power Of Tithing

Now that we had committed to God being our primary source in our financial lives, Ralph and I wanted to know everything God said about this area. It wasn't long after that God showed us this verse.

Malachi 3:8-12 (NLT)

"Should people cheat God? Yet you have cheated me! But you ask, 'What do you mean? When did we ever cheat you?' "You have cheated me of the tithes and offerings due to me. You are under a curse, for your whole nation has been cheating me. Bring all the tithes into the storehouse so there will be enough food in my Temple. If you do," says the Lord of Heaven's Armies, "I will open the windows of heaven for you. I will pour out a blessing so great you won't have enough room to take it in! Try it! Put me to the test! Your crops will be abundant, for I will guard them from insects and disease. Your grapes will not fall from the vine before they are ripe," says the Lord of Heaven's Armies.

"Try it! Put me to the test!" We took the line literally and decided to challenge God to bless us.*"If His Word is true,"* we said to each other, *"then He needs to prove Himself!"* So, we began to pay our tithe, which is 10% of all your income and increase (profit). Even though we had tithed before, this time we put a demand on God. An expectation that He would provide for us.

At that time, we had another side business that was draining us financially. Within two weeks of our decision to put a demand on God with our tithe, He gave us what we call the *"3 degree shift."* He showed us a creative business idea that had been under our noses all along. We just didn't see it. It was a slight adjustment to what we were already doing, but within a month after making it, money started rolling in again. What happened? Why were we so lucky? We understood God *had* to be the source, and God honored the demand we placed on our tithe.

Aside from not believing that God is your source, there are two other reasons why people don't see their finances prosper. First, they don't do what God asks them to do. Second, even if they are trying to obey God, they don't understand what they're doing. Let's me address reason number one first. It is true! God can only bring provision through obedience.

Malachi 3:8 (NLT)

"Should people cheat God? Yet you have cheated me! "But you ask, 'What do you mean? When did we ever cheat you?' "You have cheated me of the tithes and offerings due to me."

I know it sounds harsh, but Malachi explains that we're actually *cheating* God if we don't bring Him our tithe*! "Oh, that's not for today,"* you might say, *"That's old covenant!"* I beg to differ. Let's read verse six that comes right before eight.

Malachi 3:6 (NLT)

"I am the Lord, and I do not change."

Interesting that God says He doesn't change right before He talks about money! Hmmm. We could write a whole book on tithing alone (in fact Ralph has, and it's wonderful) but here's the basic idea. First, tithing existed long *before* the law of Moses was written. The argument that, because we've been redeemed from the law through Christ, doesn't apply to the principle of tithing. In fact, it's an argument that should never be used to get out of obeying the law in the first place.

God requires so much more from us in the new covenant than in the old. In the old covenant, it was a sin to *commit* murder. In the new covenant, it's a sin to even *think* about committing murder or hating your brother. The standard is higher, in a way that doesn't replace the original standard of the old covenant.

The death and resurrection of Christ allows us to attain salvation through God instead of our good deeds. At the same time, now that we are filled with the grace and power of God, He expects our hearts to line up with our acts of obedience to Him. We don't walk in righteousness out of fear of the law, but because our transformed hearts want to serve and please God in every part of our lives; including our finances.

First and foremost, the tithe is something that belongs in the storehouse. In today's world, the storehouse is the local church. Give your tithe to your home church, the place where you are regularly spiritually fed and cared for. Even though it's great to give to charities, evangelistic associations, or even missions organizations, your tithe should go to your home church. In our current culture online church campuses are our reality. Some people who "attend" church never actually step foot in the door of the church building. Maybe you attend church online for any number of reasons. Online or not, whether you can be seen by the preacher or not, whether or not someone sees you . . . **give**. God's principle of tithing is a basic requirement in order for Him to bless you. So make sure you give to your online church as faithfully as you would if the bucket was being passed right in front of you.

Note that *all* the tithe belongs in the storehouse. We've known people who gave God 25%-30% of their income but ended in financial disaster. For a long time, that didn't make sense to us. After further inquiry, we discovered that many of those people were only giving 3-5% to their home church. In those cases, we shared this principle, and they made adjustments. Now, they are prospering again. The moral of the story: *where* your tithe goes, matters. If you can stay obedient to God, and trust Him with your tithe, He will be the difference maker in your financial life.

Malachi 3:10 (NLT)
"I will open the windows of heaven for you."

God clearly says that, if we tithe, He will open the windows of heaven over us and pour out a great blessing. Think about this for a moment. If God says tithing will cause Him to *open* the windows of heaven over you, how were they *before* you tithed? I'm not a rocket scientist, as is my brother, but I think I can figure this one out. The answer is *closed*. If the decision to tithe or not to tithe is in our hands, then the decision to open or close the windows of heaven is also *our* decision! In short, by not tithing *you* have closed the window of heaven over your life.

Now, don't get me wrong. God is a good Father. Even if you do not tithe, He'll still answer some of your prayers for help and give you basic provision just because He is a gracious and merciful God. But, if you want to live a life that is full of everything heaven has for you, *you must open the windows of heaven!*

Malachi 3:10 (NLT)
"I will pour out a blessing so great you won't have enough room to take it in!"

I don't know about you, but, if you handed me a few billion dollars, the first thing I'd do is find a safe place to store it. Malachi says that God will pour out more than what we can take in! I am fully convinced that, even though God brings financial abundance through tithing, He also brings us spiritual blessing as well. So many times in my life I've had to literally pinch myself because of God's goodness in my life:

His love for me. His presence that touches and changes my life and the lives of those around me. Allowing me to experience overwhelming joy and peace. I believe these were all gifts from God that happened because a window to heaven had been open through our tithe. Receiving God's abundance is about so much more than just money. It's about submission, and through trust, giving God permission to bless you.

I believe tithing is a big key to having happy families, anointed ministries, great finances, and healthy bodies. It's just too risky to keep the window of heaven closed over our life. I can only imagine what would happen if 80% of our church goers across the world starting tithing. Statistically, the numbers range from 5%-25% of church goers who actually tithe. That's it. That means only 5%-25% of people sitting in church this Sunday are under an open heaven, and can obtain all the blessing and anointing that pours out from it.

So, if tithing opens up spiritual blessings, by not giving we are choking the spiritual life out of our churches. If everyone could get a revelation about tithing, God could raise up a church that would literally take the world by storm! We could be the answer to poverty and sickness; we could do outreaches that see millions of people saved! His presence would be so powerful in our services that lives would be radically touched! Tithing is not just about *"getting your money."* It's about financing God's plans for this world, and Him blessing you in the process.

Malachi 3:11 (NKJV) *"And I will rebuke the devourer for your sakes."*

Malachi 3:12 (NLT)
"'Then all nations will call you blessed, for your land will be such a delight,' says the Lord of Heaven's Armies."

Have you ever felt attacked or bullied? As if you were being backed into a corner? It's a horrible place to be. To feel helpless and afraid. How great does it feel when someone bigger and stronger than you comes to your defense? It can feel wonderful to know someone has your back. How much greater is it when you know God has your back? To know He'll protect your life! As a tither, satan loses the right to mess with your finances. He has to take his hands off your family and your ministry! He can't mess with your body! He's rebuked in the life of a tither.

A number of years ago, a woman came up to Ralph wanting to share her story shortly after hearing him teach a sermon on the tithe. She told him that, even though she had tithed for years, no one ever explained the rights and benefits that came with it.

That night, she went home and declared her authority as a tither for the first time. A year earlier, the woman's sixteen year old daughter had run away. She declared to God that her daughter would be brought back to her. That satan had stolen her daughter from her, and that as a tither he had no right to be messing with her! He was rebuked for her sake! After her fervent prayer, the next day the woman received a phone call. It was her daughter, crying, asking if she could come home!! Did you get that?? A lost daughter came home because her mother got a revelation of the tither's authority. Let's get it in our hearts that tithing is about so much more than just financing the church. It's God's way of bringing blessings into our lives.

Tithing is us choosing to put God first in our life. Money is just the tool God uses to check our heart. If He can trust us to be good stewards, He can trust us with more.

Here are five things tithing does for us:

1. It opens the windows of heaven.
2. It pours out a spiritual blessing.
3. It pours out a financial blessing.
4. It protects your livelihood and possessions.
5. It's the only place you can test God!

Every time you tithe, you cut the head off the spirit of greed. It's not money that is evil. It's the *love of money* that is. And tithing eliminates it.

There's a tithing principle I want to make very clear. It's easy to believe we are "earning" God's blessing by paying our tithe. This is a dangerous assumption to make. Nothing we do can earn anything from God. Jesus took care of all of that on the cross. It's by His grace that we freely receive God's provisions.

So why tithe? Here's the best way I know how to explain it! Ralph and I have four boys. Because we want to make sure they're taken care of long after we're gone, we have set up a series of Trusts that they will inherit in the future. When a trust account is set up for a child, it's filled with money and assets that they did not earn. Even so, some day, that child will have access to the Trust and its content. They didn't *earn* it, but because, we as parents, want to bless them, they'll be able to *access* it.

Now, each Trust has a unique set of stipulations that the child has to meet in order to gain access. They must be a certain age, use the money only in a certain way, and/or receive certain amounts at different times. There are things *they* are required to do in order to obtain the legal rights to access the Trusts' contents.

The same is true with the blessings of God. We don't receive God's blessings because we earned it. However, it's through the obedience of the tithe that we access it. The blessing is a free gift, but the obedience to tithing is the key that unlocks it.

Let me assure you that you and I can never out-give God. There have been seasons where things were tight financially for us, but ever since we started to understand tithing, we have *never* gone without. God has always showed up right on time, with exactly what we need.

Stories That Will Inspire You

Over the years, I have heard and seen so many incredible stories of regular people applying the tithe and getting incredible results. Here are three of my favorite that will encourage you towards practicing tithing in your own life!

The Young Couple

Just recently, a young couple who were brand new Christians, and expecting their first baby, attended our Victorious Living Class at church. After hearing about tithing, they took a leap of faith and started to give ten percent. At first, it didn't make sense to them. With a baby on the way, money was tight. They didn't have much to spare. Even so, they knew they had to stay obedient. Only two days after they started tithing, a relative called and told them they wanted to furnish their entire nursery! Not on a budget, either. They wanted to buy the very best of everything. Wow! What they were being given far exceeded the small amount of their tithe.

You might be saying at this point, *"It would have happened that way anyway."* That's where the story gets better. The family member who gave the furniture was not on good terms with the couple beforehand. Not only did they get the miracle of a new nursery from tithing, but it also brought the restoration of a family relationship!

The Woman In Debt

There was a woman who was far behind in bills. Her debts kept mounting. In the middle of her financial crisis, she worked up the courage to start tithing. Her tithe wasn't very much. But that didn't matter. God saw that she was obedient. Two months later she shared with me that something miraculous happened. Even though nothing big changed within her current situation, debt was being reduced! Somehow, God made sure they had enough for their bills. And slowly but surely, they started to catch up!

Sometimes you can't explain how God does it. He just does. Somehow the 90% that's left, goes farther than it used to. Things don't seem to break down as much. Extra expenses don't come around as often. God made a way where there was no way for this woman. Why? Because, even in the midst of her crisis, she was obedient!

The Businessman

Recently, Ralph and I met with a group of business people who were a part of our church, to see if we could help each other find new ways to grow our businesses and personal finances. One of the men in the group shared a story about tithing. For a long time, he had been adamantly opposed to tithing. But his wife kept insisting that they should. So, reluctantly, he finally complied. He was the owner of a franchise for a large national company. He could spare the money if it meant keeping his wife happy.

Almost immediately, after he began to tithe, his business began to grow. A short time later, he was offered another franchise territory to own. Quickly, he bought it. The business kept growing. Then it happened, again! He now owned three territories and was making triple the money. It was a miracle!

It all happened in under two years of faithful tithing. A few months ago he jokingly told us that he was getting to the point where he couldn't "afford" to tithe anymore because he had no more room for the blessing!!

Proverbs 3:5-6 (AMP)

Trust in and rely confidently on the Lord with all your heart
And do not rely on your own insight or understanding. In all your
ways know and acknowledge and recognize Him, And He will make
your paths straight and smooth [removing obstacles that block your
way].

Tithing will simply NEVER make sense in your head. It's a trust issue, and God is simply asking us to take the leap.

If you would like to learn more about tithing, Ralph wrote an amazing book on tithing called *"Anointed to Prosper."* It's a quick but powerful read that explores the topic of tithing in depth. Contact us if you'd like to get a copy!

8

ACCESSING YOUR INHERITANCE

There's something bittersweet about inheritances. The sweet part, of course, comes in the money or assets you receive. It's also bitter because someone has most likely died. A lifetime of frugal living, wise investments, and careful planning, all leads towards saving an inheritance that you can leave for your loved ones.

I heard an old story about a man who was never generous. Every penny he ever made he saved, never giving to the poor or needy. He organized his life around fulfilling his desires, and because of it, didn't have many friends. The man eventually died leaving a large estate. But on his deathbed, he made his wife promise that she would bury all the money with him.

Wanting to honor his wishes, she struggled with the dilemma presented to her. On the one hand, she did promise him she would do it. On the other, if she buried him with all his money, she would be penniless. After careful deliberation, she decided to follow through with her promise. So, she took every penny he had and transferred it all into a bank account. She then wrote a check, made out to him, for the full amount and put it in his coffin.

Long story short, his wife was a VERY smart woman! All humor aside, the rich man clearly had no comprehension of what it meant to leave an inheritance. God, as our Good Father, is nothing like the rich old man. Jesus lived a life that was worthy and sinless and then died for us. Through his death, He left each of us an inheritance.

Romans 8:17 (AMP)

And if we are [His] children, then we are [His] heirs also: heirs of God and fellow heirs with Christ [sharing His inheritance with Him]

God is a loving Father who wants to take care of us. The idea that God wants His children living in lack is just not correct. The Bible says God has blessings stored up for us that we're not even aware of! I've heard stories, in fact, there are even reality tv shows that follow lawyers hunting people down to give them inheritances they didn't know they had! Wouldn't that be cool? To find out you have a wealthy relative who left you a small fortune?

Well, I'm here to tell you today that all of you have an inheritance left by your heavenly Father. It's there, even if you didn't know it was. As a result of you not knowing, you might not have even tapped into it yet! Don't get me wrong; it's not that God hasn't provided for your needs in the past, you just haven't learned how to tap into that provision of supernatural overflow that comes with inheritance.

The good news about God's inheritance is that you didn't have to earn it.

Galatians 3:18 (NLT)

For if the inheritance could be received by keeping the law, then it would not be the result of accepting God's promise. But God graciously gave it to Abraham as a promise.

It's the same as the Trust account we discussed in the last chapter. You don't have to earn it. All you have to do is learn how to access it. I've heard of many wills that had conditions attached to them; conditions that needed to be met before the beneficiary could receive anything. God's inheritance works the same way.

Ephesians 5:5 (AMP)

For be sure of this: that no person practicing sexual vice or impurity in thought or in life, or one who is covetous [who has lustful desire for the property of others and is greedy for gain]--for he [in effect] is an idolater--has any inheritance in the kingdom of Christ and of God.

It's pretty clear. Living outside of God's principles will disqualify you from receiving His inheritance. God of course still loves you, and you may even still make heaven. But you won't receive the full inheritance that God desires to give you while still on earth. *"Wow! If God really loved me, He'd let me have it anyway!"* No! If God really loves you, He won't give you what you're not ready for. An inheritance from God is a big blessing. It goes way beyond meeting your daily needs. It's about overflow and abundance; having more than anything we could ever earn or deserve. But God reserves it for only those who are *ready* to receive it.

It's so sad every time it happens, but Ralph and I regularly hear about people winning millions of dollars in the lottery who, in just a few years, end up worse off than when they started. Why? Because their hearts and minds were not ready to be responsible stewards of such a large amount of wealth. They lacked the knowledge and discipline of how to handle it.

Money is not the automatic answer to every issue in life! It's one of those things that amplifies what's in our heart. If greed and lust are in your heart, your money will help you feed those desires. If God's purposes are in your heart, then you'll use your money to help the needy, build the church, and love people. If my eight-year-old came up to me and asked me to give him the keys to the car so he could visit gramma, would I say yes? Absolutely not!! Why? Because I love him and I know he's not yet ready for the responsibility. Even though visiting gramma's is a great thing to do, he's not ready to do it on his own. Someday he will be ready, but that day is not today! God wants to make sure we are ready for the blessings He has for us. He needs to be able to trust our hearts.

If you want to know if you're ready for God's inheritance, ask yourself, *"Have I been obedient to God in the area of my finances?"* In the previous chapter, we talked about being obedient to God with our tithes. In this chapter, I would like to talk about how God also calls us to be obedient with our offerings.

Offerings

An offering is what we give financially above our tithes. Tithing is what opens the windows of heaven, but it's our offerings that determine the overflow. The order of offerings coming after tithing is necessary. You won't receive a blessing from your offering if you did not pay your tithe first. A closed window will never allow an outflow, no matter how much you may believe or pray for it. The window has to be opened first. The two go hand in hand. Not following this principle can leave you feeling like God's word doesn't work in your finances.

Luke 6:38 (NIV)

Give, and it will be given to you. A good measure, pressed down, shaken together and running over, will be poured into your lap. For with the measure you use, it will be measured to you.

"With the measure, we use." So, if we give generously, we will receive generously. If we give sparingly, we will receive sparingly. In other words, the more you give, the more you get!

2 Corinthians 9:6-7 (NLT)

Remember this—a farmer who plants only a few seeds will get a small crop. But the one who plants generously will get a generous crop.

Our seeds in today's world are our finances. And just as a seed has to be planted before it can be harvested, we must also "plant" our finances into God's system if we want to get a return. Leaving a seed inside your packet won't get you a plant, and neither will it bring you God's financial blessing. Praying for it is also not enough. You have to release it to receive it!

Galatians 6:7 (NLT)

Don't be misled—you cannot mock the justice of God. You will always harvest what you plant.

God's principles are like gravity. Whether you believe in them or not, they work. He is a just God that *must* honor the principles He has put in place.

A Cheerful Giver

Let's clarify something that we Christians often get wrong. God requires that we tithe. He even tells us to test Him with it. I don't know about you, but if I'm testing someone on something, I usually suspect something about them and might not have the best attitude about it. God wants us to have a good attitude about giving, but with the tithe it's not required. Good attitude or bad, we are still required to tithe. The offering, however, is different. The offering is all about obedience and the attitude in which we give. God doesn't want just obedience, as with the tithe, He wants our hearts to be in it as well.

2 Corinthians 9:7 (NLT)

You must each decide in your heart how much to give. And don't give reluctantly or in response to pressure. "For God loves a person who gives cheerfully."

Believe it or not, not every offering we make is acceptable to God. Let me give you an example. If I wanted to purchase your brand new BMW from you, I would start by making you an offer. Say I offered you $500 for it. If you had any wisdom, you'd probably quickly reject such a low offer. *"But I offered you money!!"* I say, and you reply, *"Sure! But it's not the right amount of money!"* The offer wasn't acceptable.

For an offer to be valid, it must be both offered and received. Our offerings to God work in the same way. For them to count as an offering, they must be acceptable to Him.

What makes them acceptable? Requirement number one: They have to be given with a willing heart. You can't give grudgingly or as an attempt to manipulate God into doing what you want. We have to give out of obedience that flows out of our relationship with our loving Father.

Requirement number two: An offering has to be planted in fertile soil. The Bible talks a lot about the different types of soil in which we can plant our seeds. When you sow your offering, make sure you put it in the ground God wants you to put it into. There are a lot of good causes out there, but only God knows which ones will produce fruit for you. Find a ministry where people are getting saved, where miracles are happening and where God is glorified.

Requirement number three: Always give the amount God led you to give. Anything less is disobedience, and anything more is as well. When Ralph and I discovered requirement number three, it was a real turning point for us. I shared this story in an earlier chapter but it bears hearing again. At the time, we were at a church that was in the process of raising money for a new building. Even though we had experienced recent breakthroughs in our finances, we still weren't rolling in the dough, so to speak. On top of our tithes we were giving small offerings here and there, but nothing too substantial. Eventually, we each decided to pray about how much we should give towards the building campaign. After we had prayed, Ralph asked me how much I thought we should give. At first, I didn't want to tell him the number. I wanted him to say his number first. Ralph told me later that he felt the same way I did. God had given him a number that was way higher than he was expecting. He asked me first, hoping the number God told me was lower!

Anyway, I told him my number. It ended up being exactly the same as his . . . $50,000. It was way more than we had in our bank account or believed we would be able to save over the next year or two, never mind over the next few months. Even so, we knew we had heard from God. So, we decided to go all in. If we committed to the Lord, we knew He would provide a way.

It was unbelievable how over the next two months, God supernaturally pulled off some large real estate deals that provided the funds we needed!! Shortly after, we gave the money to the building fund. With that seed in the ground, the next two years took us into a realm of financial abundance that we had never experienced before. He stretched us in a big way, but we are forever grateful that He did. What our experience taught us was that God often asks us to give something that will hurt, so that He can give us something even greater in return. The greater we have to step out in faith, the greater the reward He releases. Don't wait 'til you can afford it before deciding to obey Him in the realm of offerings. Obey Him now and watch Him open up a whole new realm of blessing in your life.

Receiving Our Inheritance

In the last chapter, I shared with you the profound revelation that God is our source for everything. In a culture that celebrates personal ambition and independence, it can be a hard lesson to learn.

When Ralph and I got married, he gave me a beautiful engagement ring that was a one karat diamond in a custom setting we had designed. I still love that ring! But about 12 years ago I picked up a cheap fake ring that was a three-karat princess cut diamond that I wore on my right hand. I off-handedly told Ralph, *"Some day I'd love to have a real diamond like this,"* and left it at that. In my mind, I figured it would take fifteen to twenty years for us to get a ring like that. Little did I know that only two years later, while our family was on a cruise, it would happen.

Before we arrived at the port of St. Thomas, we had heard the island was one of the best places in the world to buy jewelry. We didn't pay too much attention to the buzz about it because we didn't plan on buying any. After taking a tour of the island, we eventually made our way into town. As we killed time, we checked out a few jewelry stores that were near the ship.

Well, wouldn't you know that the first jewelry store we walked into had a diamond ring that looked exactly like the fake one I was wearing. After showing Ralph, he laughed. They were literally the same! Exact shape, size, and the most spectacular color and quality. It was beautiful.

If any of you have ever been to the Islands, you know how hard the shop keepers work to make a sale. It didn't take long for the sales associate to start working over Ralph about buying this ring. I laughed because the price was way too high. I knew a new diamond ring was not a part of our plan at that point.

The funny thing, though, Ralph was not walking away. He kept joking about buying it, trying to gauge how bad I wanted it. Typically, Ralph would not have given the sales associate any attention. I couldn't figure out why he seemed like he was considering it. Eventually, we left the shop after a feverish negotiation. As we browsed a few more stores, Ralph started dropping hints he wanted to go back to the first store.

Long story short, the two started negotiating again. Ralph would give him a ridiculous offer like $1, and then they would go back and forth again. Eventually, the sales associate turned to me and said, *"Tell your husband how much you love the ring and ask him to buy it for you."*

As soon as I heard those words, I knew I couldn't do it. Don't get me wrong! I loved the ring. But I also knew we had no plans anytime soon for a new ring. Because it was an impromptu consideration, I would never want Ralph to regret buying it for me later on. That would take the joy out of the whole thing, for both of us.

I knew right then and there, if God wanted me to have this ring, God Himself would speak to Ralph about it. It would have to be a God idea, not a Joanne idea. I told Ralph, *"I love the ring, but I will not ask you for it. If you buy it for me, I'll love you. If you don't buy it for me, I'll love you just as much. I will not make this decision. It's yours and yours alone to make, and either way, I'll never hold it against you."*

As we left the store, I walked away from it. I made no plans to mention or hint at it again. Girls, we're really good at hinting! But if it were to be God, it had to be God fully. No manipulation. No guilt!

Once we were back on the ship, Ralph asked if I'd go ashore with him again. I had no idea why he wanted to, but I agreed. He took me back to the jewelry shop and started talking to the owner once again. I could tell He still wasn't planning to buy the ring at that price, but then the owner dropped a bomb on us. He said that he would sell it to us below cost! For some reason, even though it was the most beautiful ring he had, it had been sitting on his shelf for two years! Everyone looked, but for some reason, no one ever bought it. He joked that it might be cursed!

And there it was! It was two years ago I had said to God that I'd love a ring like that. And for two years, God held this ring for me. At that moment, Ralph knew it wasn't even a ring from him to me, but a straight gift from God! Ralph was just happy he had the honor of being the middleman for it. That afternoon in St. Thomas, he bought the ring, and it has been a joy to us both. No regrets.

If I had pushed and made Ralph my source, the outcome and the story would have been very different.

It's true; God wants to bless us. But let's stop trying to look to man for the results. Your boss isn't your source - God is! Don't get mad at your boss if he didn't give you a raise. Take it to God! Inheritance is all about realizing that God is our source, and man is merely the vessel he uses to deliver it.

The Loaves & Fishes Anointing

Almost two years after we started our church and five moves to different buildings, we were driving to a conference in Ft. Lauderdale, Florida, praying about how to find a more permanent building solution. All of a sudden, God put the story of the loaves and fishes in my spirit. I turned to Ralph and said, *"I've got it! It's the story of the loaves and the fishes!!"* Once I said those words, God's presence filled the car. There was such a heavy glory of God. Ralph responded by saying, *"You're right! But what does it mean?"* In my most sincere yet confident voice, I said: *"I haven't got a clue, but it's definitely the answer!"* Well, we had no idea what it meant, but we knew God wanted us to dig in and find out. So we did. Let me share with you what happened.

Mark 6:35-44 (NKJV)

When the day was now far spent, His disciples came to Him and said, "This is a deserted place, and already the hour is late. Send them away, that they may go into the surrounding country and villages and buy themselves bread; for they have nothing to eat." But He answered and said to them, "You give them something to eat." And they said to Him, "Shall we go and buy two hundred denarii (more than half a year's wages) worth of bread and give them something to eat?" But He said to them, "How many loaves do you have? Go and see." And when they found out they said, "Five, and two fish." Then He commanded them to make them all sit down in groups on the green grass. So they sat down in ranks, in hundreds and in fifties. And when He had taken the five loaves and the two fish, He looked up to heaven, blessed and broke the loaves, and gave them to His disciples to set before them; and the two fish He divided among them all. So they all ate and were filled. And they took up twelve baskets full of fragments and of the fish. Now those who had eaten the loaves were about five thousand men.

Some key things in here caught our attention. First off, Jesus performed His miracle out of compassion. He wanted to meet a very tangible need–feed a hungry crowd! I believe that if we want to operate in the full blessing God has for us, we need to allow ourselves to also act from a place of compassion. For our community, our cities, our nation, those who are abused and tormented. Often, we get too caught up in the busyness of life that we forget about the pain and suffering of those around us. If you want to see a loaves- and fishes-type miracle, start praying for the needs of those around you. At the same time, be willing to do something about it. For God's blessings aren't just for you, they flow through you for others.

The second thing Ralph and I noticed was Jesus took an offering. Say what?? Well, he did! He "passed the bucket" so to speak and came up with five loaves and two fish. I have to say that, for many pastors today, if we "passed the bucket" to thousands of people and all that came back were five loaves and two fish, they would dedicate the entire next month of Sundays to the importance of giving.

Whenever I read this story, I am convinced that in the crowd of 20,000 people, there were a lot of folks who had food with them but didn't give it to Jesus. Why? Because they didn't trust Him enough to give it up. Even though He preached well, and did some cool miracles, there were probably a lot of mothers who weren't about to give up the food they had brought for their families. Even so, what I love is that Jesus didn't speak to their doubt or their resistance to sharing or giving. Instead, He took what He was given and did something spectacular with it. If we want this kind of multiplication in our lives, we can't afford to step into manipulation. If God is our source, then people are not. You can only have one source - you'll have to choose for yourself whether it will be God or man.

Right before Jesus multiplied the food, He prepared the crowd by dividing them into groups. Isn't it interesting how even before Christ performed the miracle, He was already acting as if it were done. Hmm . . . Sounds a lot like the action of faith we talked about in earlier chapters! I'm sure the people were wondering what was going on. The disciples still weren't in on the plan either! They just did what Jesus asked of them. But Jesus knew what He was doing. That's why He was preparing for His miracle; acting as if it were about to happen.

What Jesus did next profoundly showed the reality of inheritance. First, Jesus went to His Father and asked Him to bless the food. Being in right standing with God, Jesus was confident His Father would meet the need. Notice Jesus didn't beg and plead. He knew His Father would see His compassion and pour out a blessing.

When you have a good relationship with your Heavenly Father, you can have every confidence God will move on your behalf. That's what Jesus did! Once the miracle manifested, there was enough food for everyone and some left over. That's exceedingly and abundantly more! You can't wrap your mind around that kind of miracle in the natural. It takes an out of the box God to push you way beyond what you thought was possible. Maybe it's time to start believing Him for more? For some things that are way beyond normal? After all, last time I checked God also called us His sons and daughters.

The miracle of the loaves and fishes happened because of relationship. Not because the offering was big, or that the people present were so perfect. It happened because Jesus had a relationship with His Father.

That's why sin can hold back an inheritance. Even though God still loves you, sin separates you from God and from all that He has for you.

We may still be saved, but unresolved, unrepented sin eats away at our relationship with God.

When you get a revelation of how much God wants to pour into your life, your heart will so desperately long for an intimate relationship with Him that there will be no sin or worldly thing, apart from God, that can fill it. You'll no longer obey out of obligation, but out of a desire for a relationship with your Heavenly Father.

Some might say, *"Joanne, you're right. It's a great story, but you're reading way too much into it!"* That's interesting you say that. Because, a few days later, Jesus did the exact same thing and received the same results. You can read about it in Mark 8:1-8. He is trying to teach us something! Jesus is modeling something we need to catch! The foundation of any miracle is a personal relationship with our Father.

Our Story

As we prayed for a new, more permanent church building, the story of the loaves and fishes continued to speak to us. God was telling us to follow in the footsteps of Jesus. So that's what we did. We shared with our church what we had learned, and boldly declared that through only one offering, we would raise the funds we needed for a new building. Instead of fund raising, we were going to radically believe God for the inheritance provision.

Wow! After we told our church, Ralph and I knew there was no going back. As a two-year-old church, that Sunday morning we took up an offering that was $12,000. It was the largest offering we had ever taken. Once it was collected, we immediately prayed over it and began our search for a new church home.

I would love to tell you that the rest of the story came together beautifully, and that a few months later we moved into a new building. Well, it didn't happen that way!! In fact, it got worse before it got better. Over the next several months, Ralph and I looked at over a hundred different buildings. We could not find one landlord who would accept our offer or a bank that agreed to loan us money. *"This doesn't make any sense,"* we thought. But I knew we had heard from God.

Six months later we had exhausted every option. And in the middle of it all, in the week before Easter, we were given ten days to get out of the location we were in. *"Great!"* I declared! In the middle of believing for big things, we felt deserted, discouraged, and alone. Even our mentors were encouraging us to rethink our plans and revisit the idea of starting a fund raising campaign. I know you've probably experienced a similar situation of discouragement before, but boy, we got in God's face about what was going on. It wasn't that I thought a fund raising campaign was a bad idea. The problem was that we had heard so clearly from God to not do one, and we were just crazy enough to believe Him!

About a month later the shift happened. God spoke to me vividly in a dream. The exact same dream over three different nights. He told me to *"Take the land."* At first, I was kind of mad God said that, to be honest. I thought, *"Take the land?? Are you kidding me?? What do you think we've been trying to do!!!"* But after the third night, I began to pray, and God spoke to me. He reminded me that in the Old Testament when God instructed people to take land, they would have to fight for it. It was war, it was physical, and it was hard. But that's what was required to hold onto the promises God gave them. Then God took me to the New Testament. He showed me in the New Testament, that's not how we take land anymore.

1 Timothy 6:12 (NIV)
Fight the good fight of the faith.

Jesus won the fight for us! He claimed the victory in advance! Now all we have to do is fight with our faith. Wow!

For months we had strived and struggled to make things work. What God needed us to do was not try to figure it out on our own, but for us to use our faith to unlock His provision.

I caught on faster than Ralph did. It's not in his nature to let things go and just wait. Even so, over the next month, we both settled on trusting God. We stopped looking for finances or property. Instead, we focused on building up our faith. By the end of the month, a friend approached us about a church building that was for sale. We believed it was something

God wanted us to pursue. After another few months, we were able to secure the same building under contract! Even with no financing, and little money, God had made a way where there was none.

Just a few weeks before we were expected to close on the building we still had no financing or money in place. Two friends approached us, independently. They explained that, even though they didn't go to our church, God had led them to help us finance our new building! Wow! We were so excited at what God was doing!

I was very grateful that our friends had offered to help us. At the same time, I strongly believed that God's initial plan was for our church to be debt-free. They gave us early possession of our new building three weeks before the deal was scheduled to close. On the day we got the keys, both of our lenders called us and said God had spoken to them in the middle of the night about giving us the money instead of loaning it to us. Praise God!!!! After scraping our chins off the floor, and letting the shock wear off, we thanked God for being faithful to what He promised us! It wasn't easy, and it wasn't always fun. But it was worth every moment because we learned that God is faithful to fulfill His promises, and He wants us to trust Him in ways we never dreamed of before.

How Do I Make It Work?

So how do you make it work? How do you believe God for the tangible things in your life? For financial solutions? You do it with trust and obedience. In both the big things and the little. When you are faithful, you will see the outpouring. Learn to be specific with what you need from God, and make sure your heart is lined up with His heart.

I remember when Ralph and I started planning for our dream home. For ten years we searched for the right house. Every time we found one, something would get in the way, or the deal would fall apart. There were other times that we took the money we had saved for a home and had to pour it into the church.

I felt frustrated for a long time. I almost gave up at one point. But I didn't! I kept believing, even if I had to put the dream on the back burner for a season or two. Still, I never let it go! I knew God had an inheritance for us. I also knew that we set the thermostat for our miracle. Just because the temperature doesn't rise as quickly in a room as you want it to, it doesn't mean it's not heading there! Don't go and change the thermostat! Keep it where you want it, and eventually, the temperature will catch up. The same is true when you're believing God for something. Your mouth and your faith are your thermostat!!

About five years ago God started dealing with me about being a good steward of the home we lived in. In my mind, it wasn't big enough for our large family. Even though that was true, I knew God wanted me to change my heart towards being more thankful. So that's what I did. I kept it up more, fixed things that were getting worn down, settled in emotionally, and worked towards being content.

About a year later God convicted me about cleaning up our garage. Up until that point, it was the "black hole" of our house–a three-car garage full of motorized toys and junk, with a small walkway carved through it. A year later, and no progress made in the garage, we found a house we fell in love with. It was everything we could have wanted, at a fraction of the cost. At first, it sounded like a God idea. But the owners wouldn't take our offer and refused to negotiate. Another dead end! After working through my initial disappointment, I remember the last thing God had told me to do. Clean the garage. So that's what I did. It was a tough job that took days, even with the help of our whole family. About three quarters of the way through the cleanup process, we got the call. Weeks after rejecting it, the sellers now wanted to take our offer! Miracle after miracle happened over the next month, and the home became ours at an unbelievable price.

"How lucky!!" you might say. I don't believe it was luck. Faith that doesn't quit will always produce. And as we learn to obey the little insignificant things as much as we believe for the big, God will pour out His blessing and provision over us.

Before we move on, I want to reiterate that financial blessing and prosperity always happens for a purpose. Yes, God wants you to be comfortable. But if that's what it's all about for you, you've missed the main event. God wants us blessed so that we can be a blessing to others. That's how

God's glory and power are displayed. Once again, it's about keeping God as our source.

I want to share one more story with you. A couple of years after God gave us a miracle for our church building, we went through a season of real financial difficulty in our church. We were way behind with bills. Ralph and I had to put in money to make sure our staff was paid. It was the first time in ministry we felt as if God wasn't showing up for us. So, naturally, we started to doubt ourselves, wondering if we were doing something wrong.

A great friend of ours who is very wealthy strongly encouraged us to let the rest of our congregation know about our financial problems. That there were bills to pay and payrolls to meet. He said to us, *"If the church doesn't know the need is there, how can they meet it?"* People give to specific projects because they see a need. It was tangible. His approach was very different from anything we had been doing up until then.

To say it felt it was the wrong decision, was an understatement. I could feel the tension in the room as Ralph explained our situation to the congregation. It didn't feel like a God idea! Well, the offering that came in was a quarter of what it typically was. Really?? *"We put it out there, and they held back their finances? Don't they care?"* Our minds were reeling about what had just happened. Weren't they all supposed to hear the need and want to save the day? We had been told that people give towards opportunities where they feel like they're adding value. But when we put the need out there, they ignored it.

Ralph is a no-nonsense guy, to say the least. After that service, he went to God and asked Him what in the world had just happened! God clearly spoke to him. *"If you go to man, you'll get man's results. If you come to me, you'll get my results. If you need something, I'm the only one you need to come to."* Talk about getting smacked in the face by God!

There it was. We had slowly drifted off course. We thought we had been trusting God, but we hadn't been. Ralph immediately repented and asked God to forgive him. We then and there promised not to take "need" before the church unless God specifically told us to. (There have been times since then that God has told us to do that, and He provided power-fully through it.) We asked God to be the source for this dilemma.

Within the next 30 minutes, there was a knock on the church office door. It was one of our church members who was a new Christian, and who had not been in the service that day. He took Ralph out to his truck, pulled out a huge wad of cash, and handed it to him. He told Ralph that it was his life's savings. God had told him to give it all away. It was $20,000. We received a miracle that day, but so did the man who gave us the money. Later he told us that his decision to give away his money set him free from the bondage of greed.

If my experience taught me anything, it's that God can move on hearts in ways we never could. The story doesn't end there. Later that week an-other man, who regularly donates to our church, but does not attend, sent in a check for $50,000. Not only did God meet the need, but He did it in God style!!

God can move on the hearts of people. When we try to manipulate or push our agenda into reality, it can get ugly. But when we trust God and let Him move on the hearts of people, we all win. We serve a God who wants to be your source for everything.

9

YOUR THOUGHT LIFE & HEARING GOD

Do you know that your future can be predicted by what's currently in your thought life? Every day we play out a multitude of scenarios in our heads about all kinds of things. I believe, for many of us, our thought life is one of the most undisciplined areas of our lives. Thoughts are so powerful that they can dictate the success or failure of our future. Depending on what you're thinking about right now, that can either be a great thing or pretty terrifying!! Society has bombarded us with all kinds of unGodly thoughts and images. Culture has convinced us that we have the right to think these thoughts and images because they're harmless. That, as long as you don't act on them, there's no harm in it. However, nothing could be further from the truth.

God has a lot to say about our thought life. Let's start by explaining what Jesus says in the Sermon on The Mount.

Matthew 5:27-28 (NLT)
"You have heard the commandment that says, 'You must not commit adultery.' But I say, anyone who even looks at a woman with lust has already committed adultery with her in his heart.'"

Wow. That's some pretty heavy stuff. Jesus explains that in order to be guilty in Old Testament times, you had to "do the deed." But now, because of grace, even just thinking about it makes us guilty. Keeping the words of Jesus in mind, I would have to say that our thought life is pretty important! God doesn't want our good behavior to be like a dog who has learned all the right tricks. He wants our whole being, including our mind and thoughts to be redeemed.

Matthew 22:37 (NIV)
Jesus replied: 'Love the Lord your God with all your heart and with all your soul and with all your mind.'

God wants your heart, which is achieved through a relationship with you, but He also wants all of your mind as well! He also doesn't want to share it with the devil or the world. God wants it all to himself. It would be so nice if, when we accept Jesus into our lives, we could hook up a spiritual super capture to our brain that would let God automatically wipe and reprogram us. That would be so sweet! But it's not like that.

Our God is a relational God who gives us free will to choose how to live our lives. At the moment of our salvation, even though our spirit man is awoken, our minds are still stuck in the way we used to think. It's in bad need of a tune-up! All our memories, habits, and experiences are still in there. That means many of us still have a lot of work to do!

So God wants your mind, regardless of the state that it's in. You're probably thinking, *"If you only knew what shape my mind was in, how much garbage is swimming around in there, you'd know I'm pretty sure God doesn't want it."* Well, God does want it! Scripture tells us that all of us are welcome to come to God, *"just as you are!"* He wants to transform your thoughts, to teach you His ways and free you from the bondage of the world.

Isaiah 55:8 (NLT)
"My thoughts are nothing like your thoughts," says the Lord. "And my ways are far beyond anything you could imagine."

Our minds are a product of what has been put in. We've heard it said before, but it's true… garbage in, garbage out. What's in your head, will go to your heart, and come out in your life!! If you want the amazing God-kind of life that you can only dream of, you better start thinking the amazing God-kind of thoughts!

Proverbs 23:7 (NKJV)
For as he thinks in his heart, so is he.

If you want a new output, you need new input! Our thought life is like a thermometer that sets where our life will end up. You control where it's set, and then the internal functions of its heating/cooling system go to work to reach the set temperature. The same is true in our thought life. Our thoughts set where our heart will take us.

If that's true, we need to regularly start inserting God's thoughts into our minds. To do that, you'll need to discover what they are. In every situation, learn to turn off what you think about it and turn on what God's thoughts would be. WWJD (What Would Jesus Do) is an old saying that many of us are familiar with. There's a lot of truth to it. It's the same question we have to ask ourselves every day. *"What would Jesus do? Or What would Jesus think?"* If you apply that question to your thoughts, I'm pretty sure you'll find a lot of thinking that shouldn't be in your brain anymore!

Our Autopilot
At this point, I don't want you running around in fear or condemnation thinking there's no hope!! Instead, I want you to understand how thought patterns work, as well as how to change them.

My husband Ralph grew up in a wonderful Christian home. I am blessed with such an incredible pair of in-laws. They provided all of Ralph's needs and never had to live in fear of going hungry! In fact, Ralph's parents used to have a rule when he was a child that he had to finish all the food on his plate before he left the table. Maybe your parents had the same rule! It didn't matter if Ralph was still hungry or not. If there were food still on the plate, he wasn't finished eating. But what about that God-given sense inside that says you're full and don't need any more food? It gets overridden with a higher power at that point in your life, called mom and dad.

After Ralph told me about the rule he had growing up, I started noticing that he still did the same thing today. Even if he were full, he had a hard time leaving food on his plate. Over the years he has gotten better at not overeating, but still admits he struggles. It's just incredible how something he learned as a child has shaped his entire adult life. The lesson: the way you were raised will often override the God-given intuitions and thought patterns you should have.

We're Taking a Trip!

Girls and guys, we're going to New York!! If you meet me at the Sarasota, Florida airport tomorrow morning, I'm going to fly you to New York on my charter plane (which for the record is an imaginary plane – and trust me, you don't want me flying it either!!). On our trip, we'll sightsee, shop, and have a great time hanging out together. If tomorrow morning comes and you decide to go with me, we will load up the jet and take off! Once the plane is in the air, I turn on the autopilot and join you in the cabin. A little bit later, I realize that we are flying west, not north! As I take back control of the airplane, I turn us around to get back on course. But again as soon as I leave the controls again, it starts heading west!! Why?? After further investigation, I realize that the autopilot is set to fly to Phoenix, Arizona. Unless I change the autopilot, every time I take my hands off the controls, the plane will veer again towards Phoenix. It doesn't matter what my desired location is. As long as the autopilot has a set direction, the plane will head somewhere else.

Let's apply this analogy to our lives. Our autopilot is the way we were raised to think. It's the collection of all the things we believe. We can try and take control of our lives using willpower, as with my example on the plane, but the moment our willpower runs out the autopilot kicks back on and changes course.

What does your autopilot tell you about your life? That you're unworthy? That you're not smart enough? That a great life is only a fantasy? That God is out to get you? That God makes you poor and lowly in order to stay humble? Those most definitely are not what God says about you or your God-given destination. We've got to get rid of and renew faulty thought patterns and doctrines that we've been taught. Willpower and hope are not enough to override the thoughts in your life. Whatever your autopilot is telling you about yourself, you have to reprogram it to say what God says about you. When you do that, you'll start heading towards where God wants you to be. Once you're reprogrammed, you can take your hands off the controls knowing that you're heading in the right direction. It will be easy.

So how do we reprogram the autopilot of our thinking? The only way to renew your mind is by reading the word of God.

Out With The Old

The old saying "Out with the old, in with the new" rings true here. In order to develop new ways of thinking, it's our responsibility to take hold of our thoughts. You make the *choice* of what to think. And that means getting rid of the stuff that's holding you back.

Philippians 3:13-14 (NLT)

No, dear brothers and sisters, I have not achieved it, but I focus on this one thing: Forgetting the past and looking forward to what lies ahead, I press on to reach the end of the race and receive the heavenly prize for which God, through Christ Jesus, is calling us.

In Philippians Paul teaches us to forget the past, and focus on the future. It doesn't happen automatically. Paul had to focus on it. In other words, we need to be intentional. I love that Paul admits he hasn't achieved it yet. We're all a work in progress! While that's true, we still need to focus and strive towards it.

As pastors Ralph and I have spent a lot of time walking people through tough life situations. One of the biggest pitfalls we see people struggle with is letting go of the past. They're so focused on their previous hurts, failures, mistakes, regrets, and even past glory days, that they stop looking forward. They end up living like they're driving down the street, only looking in their rearview mirror!! Please, for goodness sake, don't drive down *my* street doing that. You're bound to crash!

You can't move forward in life if you're only looking backwards. Just as a rearview mirror, our past should only be thought about as a teaching tool that can better help prepare us for our future. It's okay to take quick glances back, but don't put your whole focus on it. People who only look back are often the ones who struggle with condemnation. Romans 8:1 tells us that *"there is no condemnation for those that are in Christ."* As Christians, we have brought past issues to Christ and asked for forgiveness. For us, they are gone. Our past sins don't apply anymore. God has forgotten them… it's the devil that doesn't want you to forget. *"But maybe God's trying to teach me something through it,"* you may say. God can take any situation in our life and use it for good, as long as we surrender it to Him! But condemnation is not part of the process! What's forgiven is gone!!

Let's break it down: Condemnation is in your past, conviction is in your present, and hope is in your future. There's nothing you can do to change the past; that's why once you've asked forgiveness God will not remind you about it. The devil is the one who wants to condemn you. Conviction is about what is *currently* in your life that you need to learn in order to change. If you feel convicted, the answer is easy. Repent and fix it! God is obviously trying to move you into something better. Hope is always about your future. Thank goodness God is a God of hope.

Paul talks about living a Christian life as running a race. If you've ever run a race, one of the first things they tell you is to avoid looking backwards. It will slow you down. Instead, focus on the prize at the end of the finish line. In the race of life, the more we look back, the more it slows us down. You have to forge ahead and trust that God's got your back.

We serve a God who is so much more powerful than any story or situation you came out of. Today I want to encourage you, that the God *in* you is greater than the story you came from.

The Gate Keeper

In Florida, there are a lot of gated communities. In front of many of these, sits a guard who takes pleasure in asking all kinds of questions. Sometimes they can be a little over the top. Even so, their purpose is not to drive us crazy when we're trying to visit a friend; instead it's to keep the residents of that community safe. Well guess what! Our mind is the gatekeeper to our spirit. If you want to keep your spirit pure, you have to start guarding what goes into your mind.

Guarding your mind requires discipline. You might even have to give up some things you like. But it's very important to do so!! Why? Your mind is where the assault of the enemy will happen. When the devil attacks you, he attacks your mind. And how you prepare for that assault could be the difference between life and death.

Romans 8:6 (NLT)

So letting your sinful nature control your mind leads to death. But letting the Spirit control your mind leads to life and peace.

"Oh, you're just being overly religious now," No, I don't believe I am. I have seen people go through this. I have seen two different people who were both abused illustrate this point. One chose to forget the past, forgive, and take on God's way of thinking. The other chose to meditate on the past and live in regret and pain. Both had equally tragic stories, but the one who took on God's thoughts found the freedom she needed. The other still lives in bondage, unable to break free of the trauma. Regardless of our experiences, each of us has a choice. We can choose life and overcome our pasts or we can choose death and stay stuck in bondage.

What Are You Letting In?

Philippians 4: 8 (NLT)

And now, dear brothers and sisters, one final thing. Fix your thoughts on what is true, and honorable, and right, and pure, and lovely, and admirable. Think about things that are excellent and worthy of praise.

What are you letting into your spirit? In other words, what are you putting in your mind? The kind of movies, TV, news, books, and opinions of others affect you. Are they true, pure and honorable? Or do they celebrate greed, amplify your fear, or tempt you?

"Does it really matter?" you might ask. Well, have you ever seen the movie Jaws? I dare you to watch it and, after, try to swim with me in the beautiful Florida ocean. My guess is you'll be a little more than panicked when you see the fin of a dolphin as it swims by!! Or better yet, try walking down a dark back alley after watching a horror movie. I promise, even if a stray cat meowed, you'd run for your life! What am I saying in all this? What you put in your mind will affect how you think and react to what's around you.

I learned this lesson the hard way a few years ago. Sunday afternoons are our time to just relax, so we often sit and watch movies or TV and go into total relax mode after a busy Sunday morning. During that particular time frame I really enjoyed a certain medical show. Now there was nothing particularly bad about the show. It almost entirely focused on people who were sick and how a team of doctors tried to diagnose their symptoms. At first, it seemed harmless to me. At the time, I was watching the show a **lot**. The network had been running a month-long marathon on Sunday afternoons for the past few weeks. So, I had been watching three to four hours each Sunday. Then one Sunday, as I watched the show, a horrific pain shot through my leg. I had never experienced a pain like that before, and it would not go away. Even after praying for it, a horrendous pain still kept shooting through my leg! After about an hour of horrible pain, I heard the Lord speak to me. *"If you put sickness in, sickness can't help but come out."* Ouch!!

That was it. I knew better! I was feeding my spirit sickness, so of course sickness is what came out. I immediately repented and asked the Lord to forgive me. The pain instantly went away and never returned. I also never watched the show again. My experience taught me a valuable lesson. It matters what goes into our minds.

There should be a siren that goes off when you put the wrong things in your mind. Wrong input! Wrong input! Wouldn't that make it easier?

Well in a sense there is. It's the word of God. Anything that doesn't line up with the word of God screams *"Wrong Input."* The more you know God's heart and word, the louder you will hear that siren. Be diligent. Put parameters around your life to protect your mind.

Fear

Over the course of this book, we've talked a lot about the power of faith. What we haven't talked about yet is the power of fear. Just as faith will produce results in your life, so will fear.

Job 3:25 (TNIV)
What I feared has come upon me; what I dreaded has happened to me.

Fear is a funny thing. As much as we may know that we aren't supposed to be fearful, still, we tend to find creative ways to live in fear without admitting what we're doing! We mask it under labels such as *"concern"* or *"hurt."* We say things like *"I'm not afraid, I'm just concerned."* As a mom I can really relate to this. I have four grown sons. It's a huge concern for me that they make the right choices. That they choose the right life partner who also loves God and will do right by them. There were times as a mother that I let fear grip me. *What if they go down the wrong path? What if they choose wrongly?* I thought.

God quickly arrested my thought life and revealed to me another powerful principle. Concerns that are rooted in fear and panic are never from God.

1 John 4:18 (NLT)
Such love has no fear, because perfect love expels all fear. If we are afraid, it is for fear of punishment, and this shows that we have not fully experienced his perfect love.

Concerns that are healthy will always have Godly action to it. Action that results in prayer and trust. As parents we can often let our concerns for our kids spiral us into fear. When we are in fear we end up manipulating or trying to control the situation in order to calm our own emotions. But Godly concerns will take you to your knees, where you will learn that it's okay to leave your children in God's hands. You can trust that He will cover them with His powerful presence.

That's exactly what I did. I turned the fear I had for my boys over to God, and trusted Him with their lives. As a result they have started living above and beyond anything I could have hoped for. Yes, they still make mistakes. We all do! But now I have an absolutely beautiful daughter-in-law, Molly, whom I love with my whole heart. Rachael is another dear daughter-in-law-to-be, and I couldn't have chosen better if I had done it myself. God is faithful! When we trust Him He will do beyond what we can imagine.

You can't truly live in fear and faith, both at the same time. When fear gets a hold on you, it will dictate how you respond, instead of responding out of faith.

Let me clarify. While you are living in faith, you may have *thoughts* of fear of what you are stepping into, but you disregard the fear to step into faith. Faith is not always the absence of fear, but it's the decision to override it. If you're truly in faith, you'll have peace despite the fearful thoughts that come to you. If you have no peace, chances are you've let the spirit of fear take a hold. For fear is nothing more than believing that God can't take care of it.

People often don't deal with fear as severely as they should. They chalk it up to it just being an emotion. Reality is much different. Fear isn't just an emotion, it's a spirit.

2 Timothy 1:7 (NLT)

For God has not given us a spirit of fear and timidity, but of power, love, and self-discipline.

You can't wish away a spirit. You need to take authority over it if you want it to leave you. We used to have a good friend who is now with Jesus, but while he was still alive, he was an overachiever to put it mildly. He was a medical doctor who had at least three or four degrees. He wasn't just trained in multiple areas, but was a specialist and at the top of his field in each area. Our friend was very attractive, well off, and had an absolutely beautiful family. To put it another way, his life was a resounding success! To top it all off, he also loved God and regularly served Him with all of his talents every chance he could get.

One night, while we were at dinner with him and his wife, he told us he planned to travel north to visit his extended family, and was not feeling good about it at all! When Ralph and I asked why, he said that he always felt the fear of failure while around his family. *Whaaat?? A successful doctor like him was scared he'd fail around his family?* We talked it out with him some more. Sure enough, when he was younger, his parents told him he would never succeed. Ever since, he's had a drive to prove them wrong.

As great as his ambition was, it was sad to hear, because it was rooted in fear. Every time he visited family he was taken back to the fear and shame he felt as a boy. We told him about how fear was a spirit, and how it was never meant to control him the way it did. After dinner, we prayed for him. Later that day, his fear broke off of him.

After that, he traveled up north, had an amazing time with his family. For many years after that, he walked free from fear. Fear is a real thing! If you want to overcome it, you have to take authority over it. When you realize how much God loves you and you accept His powerful protection over you, you'll be able to drive out the fear in your life.

Thoughts, Imaginations and Strongholds

So, now we've determined that your thought life will indeed affect your future. You've also learned the importance of living with Godly thoughts. The question now is, *"how do I break the cycle of these thoughts?"* Maybe you've spent your whole life thinking a certain way, and don't know what steps to take in order to change. Let me explain the process.

The first thing to happen is that you get a thought. We've all had them. A thought can come out of nowhere, often about something really stupid. Then we start thinking about that thought, and might even meditate on it. *What if that actually did happen? What would happen to my life?* And on we go. Then before long we can't *stop* thinking about it. We are consumed with every possible outcome as well as overwhelmed by fear. After a while, it can feel like we're getting the very life sucked out of us. This is what we call a stronghold.

I do a fun illustration to Ralph to explain how this works. Even though *I* think it's fun, he's never quite as excited about it as I am. But I encourage you to try it yourself so you can see the power of thoughts, imaginations and strongholds. I have him put his hands together before I wrap up his wrists with a single strip of scotch tape. The tape represents a thought that comes into our mind. When I ask him to break it, it's not even an issue. It comes off easily (along with a few arm hairs I might add), and the bondage is broken. Again, I have him put his hands together. But this time I wrap it several times with scotch tape. This represents an imagination—a thought that we now let swim around in our head for awhile, thinking about how it could come to pass. When I ask him to break it, it's a bit more of a struggle (and quite a bit more arm hair), but he is still able to break free. Next I ask him to do it again, but this time I wrap him up as many times as I can. This represents a stronghold. He has taken a thought, imagined how it might look in his life, played out all the scenarios, and allowed it to take root in his life. Now it's a controlling thought in his head in his day-to-day life. When I ask him to break out of it, he can't. There's no way out. He can't break free!

This could be a thought pattern of pornography, lust, anger, hurt, fear, unforgiveness, hate, jealousy, or a multitude of other thoughts. Let me give you an example to explain what I'm saying. Let's say you find a mole on your arm that you didn't know was there. Suddenly, you have a thought that maybe it's cancer. Now, instead of just assuming it's a mole, and using wisdom to go get it checked out, you start thinking about the neighbor who died last year from skin cancer. Then you start playing out the scenario in your head—maybe you, too, have skin cancer! Within just a few minutes, you start researching online, looking up horror stories about every mole in the history of mankind that turned into cancer.

But you don't stop there. Now you are *convinced* that you have cancer, and that you're going to have to spend the next year in treatment, and maybe even die. You imagine what your funeral will look like, and who would attend. Then, in your mind, you already get offended at your cousin Sally who will probably come but definitely won't send flowers!! By this point it's real to you. It's no longer a passing thought. It's become your new reality and it's owning you. Even if you go get it checked out and find it's just a mole, you won't find relief. You are convinced that the doctor missed it, or that cancer will show up in another part of your body. The stronghold consumes you.

Do you see how a simple thought, left unchecked, can turn into something within your imagination that becomes a stronghold in your life? Many of us are spiritually bound up in our lives. We might look fine on the outside, but inside we are struggling.

But there's good news. After leaving Ralph wrapped up in tape for awhile, I finally brought out a pair of scissors, and easily cut him loose. The scissors for the strongholds in our lives is the power of the word of God.

John 8:31-32 (NLT)

Jesus said to the people who believed in him, "You are truly my disciples if you remain faithful to my teachings. And you will know the truth, and the truth will set you free."

"The truth will set us free." What a beautiful promise! The truth of God's Word over a situation can set you free from the bondage of strongholds! Ask for forgiveness for letting the stronghold take root, and then take the word of God to it like a pair of scissors. For instance, with the example I previously used about skin cancer. If you are consumed with the fear of dying of cancer, pray and ask the Lord to forgive you for doubting His protection. Then, take a scripture like Isaiah 53, that says Jesus was broken so we could be healed, and speak to the stronghold in your life! When fear tries to come at you, declare to it that you don't have a spirit of fear, but of love, joy, peace and a sound mind! (2 Timothy 1:7) When condemnation and shame come at you, declare that Jesus didn't come to condemn you but to bring you life!

You can't willpower away a stronghold. Instead, you have to take the word of God and cut through that stronghold. It's the weapon we use to win our victory.

Hebrews 4:12 (NLT)

For the word of God is alive and powerful. It is sharper than the sharpest two-edged sword, cutting between soul and spirit, between joint and marrow. It exposes our innermost thoughts and desires.

His word is what will win the victory. Even so, it's still our job to learn how to use it. Of course we can't possibly control every thought satan throws at our minds. At the same time, we are responsible for how we deal with it.

2 Corinthians 10:3-5 (NLT/TNIV)

(NLT) We are human, but we don't wage war as humans do. We use God's mighty weapons, not worldly weapons, to knock down the strongholds of human reasoning and to destroy false arguments.
V.5 (TNIV) We demolish arguments and every pretension that sets itself up against the knowledge of God, and we take captive every thought to make it obedient to Christ.

We are to take every thought captive. In other words, when a thought comes at you, you are responsible to decide whether it belongs in the garbage heap or your mind. With every thought, ask yourself *"Is that a God thought?"* If it is, then it can stay. But if it doesn't line up with what God has for us, you better trash it and quickly.

A long time ago a preacher I heard once used this illustration: *It's like a man who sees a beautiful woman walk down the street. He may not be able to avoid the first glance, but he is definitely responsible for the second one.* We are not helpless people who are at the whim of every thought. We may not be able to control what comes at us, but we can sure control how we process it and what we do with it. God has given us the tools. It's our job to use them.

So if our weapon is the word of God, guess what? You better know it. Too many Christians are happy going to church on Sunday, but never open their Bible in between. You will never have the weapons you need to fight off the enemy if you don't know your word! As the only woman in my family, I have lived much of my life surrounded by testosterone. My boys are not the quiet bookworm types. Instead, they are the rough and tumble types who have kept me on my toes and my knees for many years.

For example, they all love to shoot. They love buying and collecting guns as well as shooting them in our backyard (we live in the country - no worries). They spent a lot of time learning about their guns, have even taken lessons, and love going to the shooting range. They even spend time discussing different shells, guns and targets, and are very responsible, diligent gun owners.

When I hear them discussing it all, it's Greek to me! I've never held a gun, and certainly never fired one. I could probably get by in a pinch just because I've watched them shoot so many times. But if I were put in that situation, it would be pretty scary. If a burglar broke into my house and it was up to me to use a gun to defend my family, we'd be in pretty bad shape. Why? Because I don't have first-hand knowledge about how to use a firearm. The only knowledge I do have has come from hearing and watching other people. My sons on the other hand, wouldn't hesitate. They would know exactly how to respond in a situation like that.

The same can be said using God's word. Do we have first-hand knowledge and revelation of what the word says or have we relied only on what our pastor has said? Just as it would be hard for me to defend my home with a gun that I only had second-hand knowledge of, it will also be hard to defend our lives and our minds with only second-hand knowledge of what the word of God has to say. The good news is that for as much as wrong thoughts can create strongholds in our lives, when we plant the word of God in our minds we can create strongholds of God's Word that will produce amazing results.

Renewing Our Mind

Technology: It's a love-hate relationship. We can't live without it, but when things go wrong, we can't live with it! Everything can be going just fine. We're coasting along with all our devices. When all our phones, laptops, and computers work, life can seem great. Once we find a glitch, it can feel like our world is falling apart! Have you ever had your phone freeze? Oh my goodness… you'd think life as we know it had ended. Even though it's something so small, it can impact whole areas of our lives.

The same thing can happen in life. Everything can be going fine. Then all of a sudden a glitch happens, and it totally derails everything. You feel frozen and incapacitated. Your life that seemed so simple yesterday is now incredibly complicated.

The good news is, with a phone you can just take it in and get it fixed. They run a diagnostic, reset the system and voila, it's as good as new! However, in life, we sometimes need a reboot! A reprogramming. God has a way to do that. It's call renewing our minds.

Romans 12:2
And do not be conformed to this world, but be transformed by the renewing of your mind, that you may prove what is that good and acceptable and perfect will of God.

To RE-new means to make new again. In other words, we need a reboot back to the original way God intended for us to think and process our life—back before our experiences clouded our judgment. The word "transformed" in Romans 12 means to make into a new form. As I mentioned earlier, our house is located in the country on several acres. My biggest annoyance over the summer is the amount of caterpillars that cover the house and patios. They are literally everywhere! When fall approaches, I see cocoons hanging in all the corners and crevices of my house. I've never seen so many in one place in my life. They stand as a powerful reminder of how renewing your mind works.

A caterpillar is slow and vulnerable at first. It lives a very limited life. But eventually, something profound happens after it makes its cocoon and crawls into it. A little while later the caterpillar will emerge from that cocoon as a beautiful butterfly! It's no longer limited. Now it's beautiful and can fly free! It's incredible how there is no resemblance to its former self. It's completely transformed.

This is exactly how transformation happens in our lives. As flawed human beings, we can crawl into the cocoon of God's word. As we saturate ourselves in the word of God, something supernatural starts to happen. It starts to change us. It starts to change the way we think, and how we look at our situations! As we take scripture and meditate on it, we begin to develop new strongholds of faith.

Joshua 1:8 (NLT)

Study this Book of Instruction continually. Meditate on it day and night so you will be sure to obey everything written in it. Only then will you prosper and succeed in all you do.

When we meditate on God's word, we start to see our own lives through God's eyes and not our own. We begin to exchange the way we thought in the past with God's way of seeing things. As we emerge from the cocoon of God's word, we come out completely transformed, with no resemblance to how we used to be before. As with the caterpillar, we've been made new, by the power of God's word.

I just want to take a moment to talk about meditating. The use of meditation within the New Age movement has given meditation a bad rap. As Christians, when we meditate on God's word, we aren't trying to find a higher level of thinking. Rather, we are taking the word of God and giving it focused thought and energy.

In reality, we all meditate every day! The problem is that we meditate on the problem rather than the solution. We meditate on how we will pay the bills. Or how we feel hurt or rejected. On how someone mistreated us or spoke against us. How our kids are driving us crazy. We are giving our time and thoughts to the wrong things! We're meditating on the wrong things!

God calls each of us to spend time, every day, meditating on God's Word and His solutions. Instead of worrying about bills, meditate on the fact that God said He would supply all your needs according to HIS riches (Phil 4:19). Instead of meditating on a bad diagnosis from a doctor, meditate on the fact that Jesus is your healer! What you focus on you give power to. The question is, *'are you giving power to your problems or to God's solution?'* Make a lifestyle choice to continually, all throughout your day, not just during your devotion/prayer time, to meditate on God's Word.

For as long as we are alive and on this earth, we are all targets of satan's attacks. But while we are fighting spiritual warfare, let's make sure we don't spend all our time so focused on satan and his attacks. Instead, focus on the power we have in Christ!

Jesus defeated satan. We have the victory! Yes, it's true we have to deal with attacks from the enemy. But if you spend more time talking about satan and his attacks than you do about Jesus and your victory, you are out of balance. Don't give him more credit than he deserves. Deal with satan when you have to, but focus most of your time on the victory we have in Christ.

> *When attacks and thoughts come, focus on the answer.*
> *Watch Your Thoughts - They Become Words*
> *Watch Your Words - They Become Actions*
> *Watch Your Actions - They Become Habits*
> *Watch Your Habits - They Become Character*
> *Watch Your Character - It Will Become Your Destiny*
> *(Author unknown)*

Hearing God

I often laugh at phone messages Ralph leaves for me. They typically go something like this... *"Hi Joanne, this is Ralph Hoehne calling. Would you please call me back at 555-555-5555."* I always chuckle. It's usually because he's always in the middle of making so many phone calls, he forgets it's me he is calling when he's on autopilot. To anyone else he might call, the message would sound completely normal. But to me, it's funny because as his wife, it's out of place. Why? After 26 years of marriage, you can be sure I already know it's his voice after the first word. Sometimes when I call him, he'll answer and pretend it's Philippe's Pizza or something silly like that, but he hasn't had the chance to pull the wool over my eyes yet. Why? I know his voice too well.

One of the most commonly asked questions we get as ministers is whether or not it's possible to hear God speak, and if it is, how do you do it. First of all, I want to point out that the Bible is God's written voice to us. It is the final authority and voice that trumps all other voices. Now, going to scripture is great if you want to learn about the general will of God, as in how to live in integrity, how to serve God and other great things. But when it comes to personal things such as what job to take, or who to marry, the Bible won't have an answer. To learn the personal will of God for your life, you'll need to hear the personal voice. Since God desires a relationship with you, it's important to remember that relationships are conversational and two-sided. So yes, God does indeed speak to us.

Hebrews 3:15 (NLT)
Remember what it says: "Today when you hear his voice, don't harden your hearts as Israel did when they rebelled."

So if He does indeed speak, how do we hear Him?

John 10:2-4 (NLT)
But the one who enters through the gate is the shepherd of the sheep. The gatekeeper opens the gate for him, and the sheep recognize his voice and come to him. He calls his own sheep by name and leads them out. After he has gathered his own flock, he walks ahead of them, and they follow him because they know his voice.

Sheep know the voice of their shepherd because they spend time with him. That's why they follow only the voice of *their* shepherd. In a similar way, Jesus is our shepherd, and we are His sheep. If we spend time with Him we will recognize His voice more and more. The reason Ralph doesn't need to tell me who it is, even when I can't see him, is because I know him so well! We've spent many years together. I don't have to analyze or work hard at figuring out that it's him. I know it is! Because I know *him*.

It's the same with the voice of God. The more you know Him, through reading His word and spending time in prayer, the more you'll recognize

His voice. The better you know Him, the easier it is to discover the counterfeit voice of the enemy.

At this point in our marriage, because I know him well, Ralph can't fool me, even when he tries to disguise his voice. Satan will often try to trick you into thinking that his voice is the voice of God. He'll twist scripture just a little bit, or use your own desires to push you in a certain direction by tickling your ears with exactly what you want to hear. You need to be careful! Listening to the wrong voice can lead you down the wrong path! That's why it's so important to get to know God, and spend more time with Him, so you won't be easily fooled.

The Hearing Test

"What does the voice of God sound like, and how do we know we're hearing the right voice?" Here are a few things we have learned about the voice of God. First of all, most of the time God won't speak to you with an audible voice you can hear with your ears. Only once or twice in my life have I heard the voice of God in a literally audible way. The other times it came through a thought that seemed to come from nowhere. Like when, out of the blue, you think of an old friend and can't get them out of your mind! That's probably God telling you to pray or call them. Other times it may be a gut feeling. This is especially true when God is trying to warn you. Have you ever gone to do something you know you shouldn't, and then get a gut feeling telling you not to? Well, surprise, surprise! That's something God uses to speak to us! It's your conscience, which you could also call the Holy Spirit trying to guide and direct you. To speak to you.

Here are some ground rules that will help you figure out if you're hearing the voice of God or not. Number 1: Does it line up with scripture? I don't care how much you want to believe you heard from God, if it goes against His written word, it is not His voice! I've heard so many women tell me that God told them to leave their husband and go be with another person. Sorry! Not the voice of God. God told me to move in with my boyfriend! Nope. Not the voice of God. If it hurts someone else, is illegal, immoral, or turns others away from God, it is not His voice.

2 Corinthians 10:5 (TNIV)

We take captive every thought to make it obedient to Christ.

Take every thought and word we think is from God and put it through the test. There are always multiple voices in our head. There is God's, the devil's and our own. Every thought we have comes from one of those voices. Generally speaking, our own thoughts are selfish in nature. The devil's are usually designed to hurt us or others. God's voice always encourages us to help those around us. So, if a guy cuts you off while driving, and you have the thought that you're going to run him off the road, I'm pretty sure that wouldn't pass the test of being God's voice!

Once we've made an initial determination, the process of knowing God's voice from the other voices gets easier. The more you practice it, the better you'll get to know God, and the more peace you'll have.

Philippians 4:6-7 (NLT)

Don't worry about anything; instead, pray about everything. Tell God what you need, and thank him for all he has done. Then you will experience God's peace, which exceeds anything we can understand. His peace will guard your hearts and minds as you live in Christ Jesus.

Ask God if it's Him! Tim Storey, a good friend of ours taught us this little trick years ago. When we think we've heard something from God, we ask Him, three times, if it was Him. After the first time, we'd check if we felt peace or hesitancy about it. Then we'd ask God again if it was Him. Either the peace would increase, or the knot in our stomach would increase. Then we'd ask a third time. Generally speaking, when there was increased peace, we could assume that God was indeed speaking to us. But when the hesitation or the uneasiness increased, we reconsidered and assumed it was probably not God. Or, at the very least, it wasn't God's timing for what we were hearing. God will always lead us with peace. Don't ever act on a voice or a nudge that you don't have peace about. Pray about the issue over and over, and, until you get peace, don't act on it! God loves you and wants a relationship with you. He's always talking to us. We just have to learn how to listen.

10

GOD WANTS YOU HEALED

I grew up loving God. I had never really heard anything taught about God wanting to heal us physically. On the other hand, I also never heard anyone preach that He didn't heal. The idea of a healing God was just kind of out there, with not a lot of pastors really knowing what to do with it.

Right after my birth, I experienced a radical healing after my parents and church prayed over me. There were a few others times I was healed after prayer. Even so, there never seemed to be a rhyme or reason to it. I definitely didn't have any idea how to access healing again. I knew God *could* heal, I just didn't know if He *would* heal. I especially didn't know if He would heal *me*.

I think a lot of people wrestle with the same question. Many of you have probably seen or heard about someone getting miraculously healed. Still, the question remains, could or would God heal *you*? I've shared this story earlier in the book, but I want to elaborate on it in the context of healing. My journey of finding the answer started one Sunday morning, as Ralph and I sat listening to a pastor teach about healing. Up until that point, we'd never before heard any pastor preach specifically on the topic. So, naturally, we were curious.

At the end of the service the pastor gave an open invitation to anyone who needed prayer for healing. At the time, Ralph had arthritis in his knee and was in a lot of pain. I told him to go up. At first, he was extremely reluctant. You see, Ralph's exposure to healing was very different than mine. I at least knew God *could* heal. Ralph, growing up, was taught that God *couldn't* heal. The miraculous events in the Bible only happened when the disciples were still around. The gift of healing they had was no longer available to the church anymore.

As Ralph debated with me about how he thought the whole thing was just a big hoax, I finally asked him, *"What do you have to lose?"* If it were just a hoax nothing would happen. But if God could heal, everything would change for him.

Sure enough, Ralph's knee was healed during that Sunday morning service. During the same service, something else remarkable happened.

While Ralph was up at the altar, the pastor stated that God was also healing people's eyes. In that moment, Ralph didn't feel anything special. However, later on, after we went home, Ralph took his glasses off, complaining that they were giving him a headache. Remember, Ralph had worn glasses since he was three years old. As long as I had known him, he always needed them to function. From the moment he took them off, every time he tried to put them back, he got a headache.

Being a typical man, Ralph refused to get his eyes checked. After weeks of not wearing his glasses, Ralph finally caught on to the fact that he could see perfectly fine without his glasses! Months later, when Ralph went in to get an eye exam, the doctor told him he had 20/20 vision. His eyesight had been healed!

Finding out my husband's eyes had been healed was a turning point for us. God was indeed a healer. He clearly had so much more to offer than what we had been told. Since then, it has been our life's mission to know everything we can about God. We committed ourselves to learning all we could about what God really had to say about each and every area of our lives.

The many lessons God ended up showing us over the years have been practiced by our family over and over again. Through our ministry, we have seen hundreds of people learn the gift of healing within their own lives. If you take the time to understand what God says about it, the gift of healing is yours to take, use and experience.

Healing Is God's Will

Jesus came to pay the price for our sins, but He also came to make a way for us to have so much more, as in the healing for our bodies.

1 Peter 2:24 (TNIV)

He himself bore our sins in his body on the tree, so that we might die to sins and live for righteousness; by his wounds you have been healed.

The wounds referred to in this verse are the whip lashes that Jesus took to His back. He paid a physical price for our healing. The most profound part of this verse is the words *"have been."* It doesn't say, *"will be"* healed, it says *have been* healed. That means it's already done! It's already a finished work of the cross. It's not a maybe, or a hopefully someday, if I wish upon a star kind of thing. It's done, settled, and completed because of what Jesus did for us.

Here's another profound scripture that talks about what Jesus did for us on the cross.

Isaiah 53:4 (NIV1984) *(words in parentheses ours)*

Surely he took up our infirmities (sickness) and carried our sorrows (pains).

In this verse, grief or infirmities means sickness of the body, and sorrows means physical pain. Some have tried to say that this verse only refers to our spiritual sorrow. But when you research how the verse was originally written, it clearly means physical disease and pain.

Jesus paid such a high price to redeem us. Why would he go through all the pain and sorrow of leaving heaven, coming to earth, dying a painful death on a cross and then rise again to defeat only part of what Satan has thrown at us? Don't you think that God is big enough to handle everything

in this fallen world that might come at us? I believe God is able enough
to, not only save our souls and forgive our sins, but also to heal our bodies
and give us new life in every aspect.

Jesus physically rose from the dead. It's not a metaphor. It actually
happened. He conquered death in both a spiritual *and* physical way. That's
really good news for you and me. Not only can we spiritually come to life
through Jesus, but we can also have life come back into our bodies because
of His resurrection.

Romans 8:11 (NLT)
*The Spirit of God, who raised Jesus from the dead, lives in you. And
just as God raised Christ Jesus from the dead, he will give life to your
mortal bodies by this same Spirit living within you.*

Wow! Resurrection power is available for our bodies. To understand how
much God wants to see us healed, you have to understand how much He
hates sickness. Sickness was never part of God's original design for our
lives. He hates sickness, pain and disease! God is a good God who wants
you to prosper and live in total health.

One of the biggest errors people make while praying for healing is
they add this little phrase at the end of their prayer. *"If it be your will."* I, myself, am guilty of doing this for years. As discussed in a previous chapter,
if you pray like this you haven't yet had a revelation about God as a healer.
It's always His will to heal.

I believe we include the phrase "if it be your will" to release us from
the responsibility of exercising our faith for healing. That's why I did it.
If healing doesn't happen, then it just wasn't God's will. This kind of language makes us lazy in our faith.

"Well, God is sovereign" you might say. Oh, yes He is! And in His sovereignty, God sent Jesus to die for our sins and establish a covenant of
healing that we could all tap into. In God's sovereignty, He decided how
our healing manifests. Granted, I would love if God decided that all of us
were instantly healed, but sometimes it takes us walking out our recovery
to receive it. Other times it's with the help of medical professionals. It's not

our job to tell God how He should heal us. Rather, it is our job to believe that He will.

Jesus Always Healed

Reading through Matthew, Mark, Luke and John, there can be absolutely no argument about the fact that Jesus was a healer. But I also want to point out that Jesus was *always* willing to heal. Every sickness, in every situation and at any time.

Matthew 8:2-3 (NIV1984)
A man with leprosy came and knelt before him and said, "Lord, if you are willing, you can make me clean." Jesus reached out his hand and touched the man. "I am willing," he said. "Be clean!" Immediately he was cured of his leprosy.

"I am willing." You'll find that same answer over and over and over again in scripture. In fact, I can't find a single verse that says Jesus was *not* willing. He was always willing, and there was nothing He wasn't able to touch and heal!

Luke 4:40 (NLT)
As the sun went down that evening, people throughout the village brought sick family members to Jesus. No matter what their diseases were, the touch of his hand healed every one.

It didn't matter what was wrong with them. Jesus was able to bring healing. He also didn't just heal this one, or that one, and leave the other one. He healed everyone.

Matthew 15:30-31 (NLT)
A vast crowd brought to him people who were lame, blind, crippled, those who couldn't speak, and many others. They laid them before Jesus, and he healed them all. The crowd was amazed! Those who hadn't been able to speak were talking, the crippled were made well,

the lame were walking, and the blind could see again! And they
praised the God of Israel.

He healed them all! There are many more Biblical examples that show the same thing. Jesus is the healer, and *no one or no disease* is beyond His healing grasp. The only place in scripture Jesus was unable to do any great miracles was in his own home town after the townsfolk did not receive Him. Matthew says they were "offended" with him. Even though Jesus wanted to bring healing, the people weren't willing to receive!!

How many of us aren't seeing healing in our lives because we, on some level, aren't willing to receive? Or because we harbor offense? Maybe the idea of a healing God is so far outside of the set of ideas we were raised to believe. It could also be that it all just sounds too good to be true! Even when people didn't believe, Scripture says Jesus was still able to bring healing to a few.

We've all had personal experiences that make it hard for us to believe for healing. An aunt who loved Jesus with all her heart died of cancer. A young child died in a car accident. A teenager dies of a rare disease. In life, we will never be able to explain why all these bad things happen this side of Heaven. What we can do is accept that we still live in a fallen world. We will not reach the perfection that God desires for us until we reach Heaven. At the same time, I need you to understand that God's *perfect* Will for your life is that you will experience healing in this life.

I am absolutely devastated when I hear people say *"God put cancer on someone to teach them a lesson."* The Bible talks about God as a good father. As a mother who was far from perfect, I could never in a million years put cancer on my child because he disobeyed me or needed to be taught a lesson!! That's child abuse! So why would God do something like that? He wouldn't. We live in a fallen world and battle against a very real enemy.

John 10:10 (NKJV)

The thief does not come except to steal, and to kill, and to destroy. I have come that they may have life, and that they may have it more abundantly.

Satan comes to bring death and destruction to our lives. But God wants to bring life, and abundant life at that. For too long, we have let the circumstances we were born into define our lives, instead of living by what God's Word says. What happened during your childhood is not the only truth that should shape your worldview. It is on God's eternal Word that we build our life.

In many of the verses I mentioned above, healing came in an instant. When an instantaneous healing occurs, it's a truly wonderful thing. I have seen it happen many times in my life. Every time it does, I am still taken aback at how incredible God is. Sometimes, however, healings don't happen instantaneously. In Matthew 9, there is a powerful story of a man who came to Jesus after his daughter had died. Even though the girl was dead, Jesus still agreed to go with him. Along the way, Jesus was delayed by another woman who needed healing. I could only imagine what the father was going through. If I were the parent in the story, I'd want to see Jesus running to my home, pushing every obstacle out of our way. Regardless of what the father of the dead girl would say, Jesus would stop. He was operating in his own time frame. Eventually Jesus arrives at the man's home and raises the girl from the dead. It may not have been as quickly as her father wanted him to act, but the end result was the same. She was healed.

Is Healing for Today?

Most people won't argue the fact that Jesus was a healer. But that was then, and this is now! We aren't Jesus, so we can't expect to see the same results that He did. Well, throughout the New Testament we see Jesus commissioning His disciples to pray for the sick! Even after Jesus ascended, the disciples were empowered to heal people throughout their ministries.

Mark 16:17-18 (NLT)

"These miraculous signs will accompany those who believe: They will cast out demons in my name, and they will speak in new languages. They will be able to handle snakes with safety, and if they drink anything poisonous, it won't hurt them. They will be able to place their hands on the sick, and they will be healed."

If you believe, you can also receive. Wow! You and I can see healing in our lives using this powerful truth. It's easy to challenge this point. I meet people all the time who try to convince me that miracles don't happen today. Well, I have seen the gift of healing manifest in my life dozens and dozens of times, and in the lives of those around me hundreds of times! At this point, I am not just convinced of healing, I am fully persuaded. And I pray that, as I share with you what I know, you will also become fully persuaded.

How Does It Work?

Healing happens in all kinds of ways. There is not one specifically right way to pray for healing for others. If you want to learn more about the many elements of healing, and praying for others, check out our curriculum. For this purpose, I want to break down how to receive healing for yourself into a few really simple steps: Hear, Believe, Act.

1) Hear

Romans 10:14

How will they know unless they hear?

If you don't know anything about healing, how can you get healed? We didn't start receiving healing in our bodies until someone started sharing with us that God wanted to heal us! We don't know what we don't know.

Luke 5:15 (NIV1984)

Yet the news about him spread all the more, so that crowds of people came to hear him and to be healed of their sicknesses.

Jesus usually taught people about healing before He healed them. The Word of God is alive and powerful. As we put the Word of God out before us, it starts to work in people. It prepares their spirits to receive. It raises faith, and dispels fear. It tills the soil, so to speak, of our hearts so the seed of healing can produce something powerful. When we pray for people, we like to also share what God's Word says about healing. Even if it's just a verse or two. There's power in the Word of God, and I want as much access to that power as I can get!

Proverbs 4:20-22 (NKJV)

My son, give attention to my words; Incline your ear to my sayings. Do not let them depart from your eyes; Keep them in the midst of your heart; For they are life to those who find them, And health to all their flesh.

The word health in this verse actually means medicine. The word of God is medicine to our bodies. It's easy to understand how food brings life to our bodies. That's why we eat every day. But if we also understood that God's Word brings life to our bodies as well, we would be a lot more diligent about reading scripture every day!

Romans 10:17 (NKJV)

So then faith comes by hearing, and hearing by the word of God.

It's not what you know, it's what you're hearing. That's present tense. It doesn't say faith comes from what you have heard, it says it comes from what you hear. I may have listened to a month of teaching on healing 10 years ago. But if I need healing today, that's not going to help me! It might provide a strong foundation, but it won't get me healed today, unless I take the Word of God and hear it today, so I can have faith for today.

About ten years ago I developed a mysterious illness that the doctors couldn't diagnose. For months I struggled to even walk or function in day-to-day normal activities. I would pray over myself and speak to my body, but what I wasn't doing was getting "fresh hearing" about healing.

I was relying on past input, and it wasn't working. One day I became sick and tired of being sick and tired. I sat in my car with healing CDs playing and resolved that I would not leave that car till I was full of the word of God on healing. A few hours later symptoms started to disappear, and later that night I was completely healed. It wasn't until I sat and put fresh faith for healing in my ears and in my spirit that I saw healing. The Word of God is not just knowledge. It's alive. It brings life and faith to our current situation. It's not just a text book. It's the living and breathing Word of God.

When you're going through sickness, the first thing you should be reaching for is God's Word about healing. Study how people were healed. Get good teaching from pastors who can help you better understand what healing is all about. Fill yourself up!!

In seasons when Ralph and I needed healing, we had CDs in our car and in our house. For days, they were all we filled ourselves with. We had scriptures posted on our mirrors. We spoke scriptures of healing over ourselves and our kids. We were diligent!

You can be lazy in the realm of healing and say you just don't feel like doing the work, but chances are you won't get your faith level to a place where you'll actually be able to see it manifest. You can either spend your energy being sick, or spend it getting healed. If you're sick and tired of being sick and tired, you'll be willing to dig in and seek God for answers.

2) Believe

Healing is something that is available to everyone. So, why isn't everyone being healed? Not everyone has tapped into the promise. We don't have to earn our healing, but we do have to unlock and receive it. Jesus was very clear that we unlock it through faith, or by believing.

Matthew 9:28-30 NLT

They went right into the house where he was staying, and Jesus asked them, "Do you believe I can make you see?" "Yes, Lord," they told him, "we do." Then he touched their eyes and said, "Because of your faith, it will happen." Then their eyes were opened, and they could see!

In this story Jesus declares that a person's faith has made them well. That's pretty cool! It means we don't have to wait for that special healing evangelist to come to town, or for your church to have a healing service to receive healing. If our faith can make us well, then the ball is in our court! We can grow our faith, and access healing for ourselves! What amazing news! It's our responsibility to believe. No one else can do that for us. I want to show you another interesting story.

Mark 9:20-24

So they brought him. When the spirit saw Jesus, it immediately threw the boy into a convulsion. He fell to the ground and rolled around, foaming at the mouth. Jesus asked the boy's father, "How long has he been like this?" "From childhood," he answered. "It has often thrown him into fire or water to kill him. But if you can do anything, take pity on us and help us." " "If you can'?" said Jesus. "Everything is possible for him who believes." Immediately the boy's father exclaimed, "I do believe; help me overcome my unbelief!"

Here's a story of a desperate father. Any parent who has a child in trouble knows the lengths to which they would go to help their child. That said, there's clearly doubt on the part of the father. There's an interesting shift that had to take place before Jesus went on to heal the boy. The father "hoped" Jesus could help, But he wasn't convinced by any means. His heart hoped, but his head didn't believe. Jesus needed the father's heart and head to line up for this miracle to happen! How many times are we hoping in our heart but doubting in our head? This is difficult when we're dealing with sickness. Your body is screaming one thing at you, and your heart is yearning for something more. In times of sickness, you need to speak to that unbelief and cry out for truth! Declare the truth over your situation 'til your head and heart line up.

Matthew 8:13

Then Jesus said to the centurion, "Go your way; and as you have believed, so let it be done for you." And his servant was healed that same hour.

This verse hits on a key element of healing. Jesus says, "As you have be-lieved," literally measuring the level of the miracle in direct relation to the level of the centurion's faith. Wow! Our belief system can limit God or give him a full green light. The ball is in our court. *We* set the thermostat or the level of healing we will receive. This kind of puts us in the driver's seat. It's so much easier to be lazy in our faith, to not grow our belief, and blame not getting healed on God's will. I know I'm stepping on some toes, but they were once my toes as well. I so desperately want you to under-stand that there is much more in the realm of healing if you are willing to push into it more.

We can't go beyond what we believe for. I mentioned this idea briefly when I talked about finances, but it's just as important when talking about healing. When sickness hits, we have to be honest with ourselves by find-ing out what we can *really* believe God for. For example, maybe you re-ceived a diagnosis of diabetes. If you're having trouble believing that God could heal you, but you do believe God could empower you to find the right diet and medicine. Maybe the doctor told you that you have a tumor. You might not have the faith to believe that the tumor will disappear, but you do have the faith to believe the doctors will be able to successfully remove it. It's okay to be honest with yourself about how much faith you have.

The first thing I ask a person when I'm praying for their healing is, *"What are you believing for?"* If you just want someone to pray with you that your surgery goes smoothly, in order for me to be in agreement with you, I can't start praying for your total healing. Being "in agreement" means getting another person to pray with you for the *same* result you want. Wherever your faith level might be in that moment, there is no condemnation!

Romans 8:1 (NLT)
So now there is no condemnation for those who belong to Christ Jesus.

Believe God for what you feel ready to believe Him for. That said, start growing your faith, so the next time you can believe Him for even more!

Ultimately, your goal should be to live a healthy and whole life. How we get there is not nearly as important.

Our family has seen a lot of injuries and broken bones over the years. I've always joked that I stepped into a healing ministry just by being a mom. I've had so many chances to practice! About six years ago, one of our teen sons came home from youth group with an injured foot. I had already gone to bed. When our son showed his foot to Ralph, in true dad style, Ralph said something like, *"suck it up, you'll be fine."* Great dad compassion, right?

In the morning, I finally saw his foot. It was swollen, completely black and blue. It was clear it had been broken. After breakfast, I stuffed him in the car and took him to the ER. Before praying over him, we had to agree on what we could *actually* believe God for in this moment. Not what we wanted to see! But what we could actually believe for.

We had seen so many miraculous things happen to our son's body over the years. Literally, God had given us miracles in life or death situations. However, that was then and this was now. I would love to say that I looked over at him and said *"Son, let's believe for God to restore this bone completely."* But, unfortunately, that was not where I was.

The few months prior had been a heavy season of sickness and injury. I was tired and my faith was not built up as it should have been. I honestly couldn't say, in that moment, I could believe for total healing. *"So what **could** I believe for?"* I asked myself. After talking with my son about it, we both agreed that we could believe that no surgery would be needed. There would be no complications and his foot would heal naturally, but quickly. After we agreed, we prayed for it together. After we got to the ER, and received an x-ray, the doctor came into our room shaking his head. He told us he'd never seen anything like it before. The bone in our son's foot did not just break, it had shattered into seven pieces. What was miraculous was that none of those seven pieces had moved. Every single piece was still in place! The Doctor had no medical explanation for how a foot could break in this way.

Praise God!! We got what we believed for. There's power in prayer when you can actually believe for what you're asking for. It's called faith, and it can move mountains.

Now I have to be honest with you. Even though our son had received a miracle, I wasn't happy that he had to deal with a broken foot to begin with. I got angry at the devil and once again dove into God's Word about healing. Satan wasn't going to take us out again! Two months later one of our other sons injured his thumb. Once again, it clearly looked like a break. The swelling, the dark bruising, the whole thing. After calming him down, I looked at him and asked if he'd be willing to wait 24 hours and give God a chance to heal it. He said absolutely! As a family, we prayed over his thumb right before he went to bed. The next morning, when he woke up, he was completely healed. There was not even a hint of bruising (and it had been bad), and not a stitch of pain. Praise God! We were ready.

Whenever God gives you an opportunity to stand in agreement with another, never forget that every person is in a different place in their journey of faith. Never speculate as to why someone is sick or judge them because they aren't believing for a greater miracle. As people of God, our primary job is to encourage one another. I have heard too many stories in "faith churches" of people hiding their sickness because they didn't want others to look down on them. Sometimes, people will even forgo the help they need, and end up dying or getting sicker as a result, so that people won't accuse them of not being a person of faith. That is not God's heart! He takes us as we are, and He'll meet us where we're at. We need to do the same with each other.

Mark 11:22-24 (NLT)

Then Jesus said to the disciples, "Have faith in God. I tell you the truth, you can say to this mountain, 'May you be lifted up and thrown into the sea,' and it will happen. But you must really believe it will happen and have no doubt in your heart. I tell you, you can pray for anything, and if you believe that you've received it, it will be yours."

Jesus told us that if we believe, we can speak to the mountains. If we believe He is the healer, and our healing is already done for us, we can speak to that mountain of sickness. We can command it to die, just like Jesus commanded the fig tree to die.

Now, I want to point something out to you. When Jesus cursed the fig tree, it did not look dead right away. It was the next day that His disciples discovered it had died. For, when Jesus cursed the tree, he spoke to the *root* of the tree. That died instantly. However, it took time for the branches and leaves to feel the effects of the dead root. When we speak to cancer in our bodies, we command it to die. Once we do, the symptoms can still linger. Regardless, when we receive healing, we can know that the root of our cancer no longer has a right or claim over our bodies.

This is so often where many of us miss it. We pray for healing, but because the symptoms are still there, we don't think it worked! Faith is all about believing in what you don't see. It's believing that the word you spoke over yourself is and will do the work it is supposed to do. We have to learn to look past our symptoms and circumstances and stand in what we believe God has done because His Word says it's done.

There is another point worth discussing before we move forward. Jesus didn't pray and ask the Father to kill the tree. He knew he had authority all on His own. That's why He spoke to it and saw it die. When many people pray for healing, it sounds something like this, *"Father, please heal Aunt Susie. I pray you would take away her sickness and send healing to her right now in Jesus' name."* Sounds good, right? However, it's not quite where it needs to be!

If Jesus' death already paid the price for our healing, and is now freely available to us, what more can He do? Is Christ supposed to come back again and pay the price for Aunt Susie's healing a second time? Of course not! Jesus has already done all that. The ball is now in our court. Our job, now, is to receive. It's to take the authority He has given us and speak to the mountains in our lives.

This is how I would pray, *"In Jesus' name, I command this sickness to leave Aunt Susie's body right now! By Jesus' wounds the price for sickness has already been paid and I declare right now her body healed and whole in Jesus name."* Now that's a prayer that understands our authority and Jesus already having taken care of sickness. We have to stop begging God for healing. There's nothing more He can do! It's already available. We just need to learn how to access it.

Once we've spoken to sickness, step number two is putting our faith into action. We do that when we believe we've received our healing, even when we don't feel as if we are yet. Too many people give up just before their miracle. We live in a microwave mentality culture. If it doesn't happen right away, we assume it never will. When Ralph and I first started learning about healing, we had the chance to put our newfound faith into practice during a life and death situation. When our son Ashton was about a year old, we started transitioning him from formula to cow's milk. One night he wouldn't calm down. He just cried and cried and was extremely upset. Out of nowhere, he started vomiting. Shortly after, his entire body was covered with one large red swollen hive. There wasn't a single part of his skin that wasn't a red hive. His head also began to swell. At its peak, his head was over 25% larger than normal. It was horrible. Ralph and I were both terribly frightened! After calling the local hospital, the doctor told us not to wait for an ambulance. Our son had to come to the ER now! On the way to the hospital, we watched as our son's eyes slowly rolled back into his head. His small body flopped unconscious. I honestly can't even remember if he was breathing or not.

Without even consciously realizing it, everything that God had been teaching me about healing came roaring out of me. Ralph kept driving as he watched me grab my son and shout, *"In Jesus' name you will live and not die!!"* All of a sudden he started breathing and his little eyes opened up. By the time we reached the ER the swelling had began to subside. Our son was still in serious condition, but he was alive! Later on, we discovered that he had an extreme allergy to milk, along with wheat and a couple of other things.

Well, wheat and milk are in almost everything! Despite our best efforts, a few weeks later, our son grabbed a few noodles of macaroni and cheese from his brother's bowl, and we repeated the whole episode again. Now, however, we knew this was a matter of life and death. This time, we decided to push in and believe God for this. We were strong in our faith. We knew God had this.

Of course, while we believed and prayed scriptures of God's promises over him every day, we used wisdom and protected him from any products or foods that might hurt him. We also prayed daily protection over him, that he would not come in contact with anything he was allergic to.

A few months later, with our faith at super hero level, we were absolutely convinced he was healed. We asked our doctor to retest his allergies. At first, they strongly opposed the idea, but eventually agreed.

We were not prepared for the results. They were worse than the first time he had been tested! His allergies had become so bad the test couldn't even register how severe they were. At this point Ralph and I had a choice. We could either decide that our faith had failed and accept that our son had to live with these allergies, or decide that our faith was working. That, even though we couldn't see a healing yet, things would soon have to turn around. We chose the latter. Month after month, we kept thanking God for our son's healing. We kept listening to the Word and spoke that Word over his life every day. We knew that we knew that we knew he was healed. Eventually his body would just have to catch up with our faith.

A full year later, we felt in our spirit it was time to retest him. Once again, our doctor resisted. We pushed and pushed until he finally agreed. Looking back, I think the doctor agreed to the test just so he could get us off his back! For, we were not backing down. Long story short, they redid the test four times. The reason: the test kept coming back negative for all allergies! Each time they got the results, the doctor was left scratching his head. Later on, he further explained that even when someone outgrows an allergy, trace amounts are left in their system for up to seven years. Ashton had zero traces. They actually wrote in his medical file that it was an unexplainable miracle. Praise God! Yes, it took a whole year of praying and believing. But that was better than Ashton living the rest of his life with an allergy!

Looking back, I'm grateful we didn't receive the miracle right away, because it caused us to go deep into the Word of God and truly rely on it. We had to learn how to trust Him and what He said about healing. It became our own revelation. As a result, we have seen healing in our lives and the lives of others ever since.

3) Act

James 2:20 (NKJV)
But do you want to know, O foolish man, that faith without works is dead?

For our faith to be alive and work, it must be accompanied with a corresponding action. There is always something we are required to do in conjunction with our belief for it to be faith. It takes a lot more trust in God, and can be much scarier than just saying you believe, and sitting back waiting to see what happens. It is the radical trust of acting on what we believe that God honors.

Acts 3:6-7 (NLT)
But Peter said, "I don't have any silver or gold for you. But I'll give you what I have. In the name of Jesus Christ the Nazarene, get up and walk!" Then Peter took the lame man by the right hand and helped him up. And as he did, the man's feet and ankles were instantly healed and strengthened.

"And as he did . . ." Note that before the man got up and walked, he didn't realize, at first, that he was healed. That's because his healing didn't fully manifest until he decided to get up and walk. Until he got into action. Sometimes we have to act healed in order to actually be healed. Last year, two of our sons, Brett & Connor, traveled to the Dominican on a missions trip. Our son Connor has worn glasses since he was young, and was unable to function without them. While on the flight to the Dominican, for some strange reason he got sick. He spent most of the flight throwing up in the bathroom. Once they landed, he realized that, somehow, amidst all the commotion, his glasses had broken. One of the lenses had gone missing.

"Great!" I thought after I'd heard. *"He just landed for a week-long missions trip and he can't see a thing!"* After talking with him on the phone about it, I felt something rise up in me. Here he is, in a foreign nation away from home, trying to serve God, and the devil was messing with him. *"This would be a great time for a miracle!"* I thought. After telling him that, I asked him what he wanted to do. He firmly responded with: *"Let's believe God for my vision!"* After we got off the phone, his team prayed over him.

The next day I called and asked him how he was doing. He told me he still couldn't see. Ralph and I were planning to travel to the Dominican a few days later to join the missions trip. I asked Connor if he wanted me to bring another pair of glasses for him. Though we were going to be in another part of the country, we would have found a way to get them to him. *"Mom, I don't want a backup plan,"* he responded. *"I'm healed and I'm using my faith."*

I stood in agreement with him by not purchasing and packing an extra pair of glasses in my bag. The next day—two days after losing his glasses—he woke up in the morning with perfect vision. He had received his healing!

I was so proud of my son when I heard the news. He had a choice, and he chose to use a bad situation to push his faith to another level. Instead of looking at his circumstances and settling, he chose to act as if he were healed, and God came through. That week he prayed for several people who were completely blind, and their sight was miraculously restored.

Since he shared his testimony in our church, we have seen at least three other people throw away their glasses over the last year because their eyesight was miraculously healed. Praise God! When we act as if His word is true, it's amazing what can happen.

How do we ACT?

I want to get really practical about how to put your faith into action.

A) Learn to Receive.

Don't just pray for it. It's already done! Get a revelation that your miracle is a finished work of the cross. It's not something we beg or plead for. We need to learn to receive. We don't need two years of healing school. We just need to receive. If you believe you've received, you'll start thanking God it's done!

B) Speak the Word over Yourself

We talked about this earlier. It is so important to be hearing and speaking the Word of God on a regular basis. His Word is sharper than any two-edged sword, so we need to be using the power of the Word to do battle with the sickness in our lives. Find scriptures on healing, and when you start to feel symptoms, fight back with scripture. When Satan tempted Jesus in the wilderness, Jesus responded every time with *"The Word says . . ."* He fought the devil with the Word of God. If that's how Jesus resisted evil, then we had better learn to do it, too. We can't fight without it.

C) Enact Your Faith!

Start acting as if it's already done. Start thanking Him! About a month ago, in one of our services, I prayed for one of our ushers who had pulled a muscle in his back. He was in so much pain, he couldn't even stand up straight. He had been at home recovering for most of the week. After I prayed for him, I told him as I tell everyone: *"Leave church thanking God that your miracle is already done. Your act of faith is believing that you're healed even if the symptoms are still there."*

After the service, he left still in pain. However, later that afternoon, he started thanking God that he had received, and that he was healed. All of a sudden, all pain left his back, he straightened up, and he was completely healed from then on. You see! Thanking God tells yourself and God that you have already received it. That you're not waiting for it, and it's already yours.

D) Get Rid of Any Obstacles

This is a big one. Anything we tolerate, we won't get rid of. If it's not a big deal to take a few pills every day for your condition, you probably won't push in to see if you can receive your healing. I am so grateful to live in a country with such great access to medical care. But having that access can also make us spiritually lazy. When we get sick, it's often not a matter of life or death. I believe because we have such easy medical solutions to many common health problems, it is a big part of why we don't see more healings. When you're traveling overseas in the third world, even the most basic medical treatment is often unavailable. At the same time, there are mass amounts of supernatural healings. Friends of mine who minister around the world say that foreign countries are by far the easiest meetings to witness thousands of people being healed. Why? Because God is their only option! There is no back-up plan. They've put all their eggs in one basket, and that basket is God's supernatural healing.

Another way to get rid of obstacles in the way of our healing is to take a personal inventory of our emotional needs. It can be hard to admit out loud, but sometimes we can enjoy the pity and attention we get from others when we're sick. As a child I was hospitalized for a few days. I remember hating that I was sick but loving all the attention I received! People doted on me, they brought me gifts, and everyone noticed me. If you're not careful, that kind of attention can hold you back from your healing!

I've actually met people who didn't want to be healed, because they didn't want to lose their disability insurance, or lose the compensation they'd receive because of their illness. In fact, they've even asked me to pray that their support not end! I'm sorry, but God has so much more for us than that. It's easy to fall into the trap of sitting in your setback. When you're sick, sometimes it's hard to imagine what life was like when you were healthy. As a way to cope with our suffering, we end up settling for less.

The final obstacle we must overcome is the poison of unforgiveness. I will talk about unforgiveness more in a later chapter. But for now, there is often a direct connection between the unforgiveness in your life and the sickness you endure. Holding on to unforgiveness is never worth it! Releasing your pain and forgiving another will often free up your healing.

A couple of months ago I had a woman share this testimony with me. She had a horrible pain in her shoulder for a few weeks, and couldn't figure out what happened! It felt as if she had pulled a muscle but couldn't figure out how or when she did it. During one of our services we talked about the importance of forgiveness. As she was listening, God reminded her of someone who had recently offended her, and whom she had not fully forgiven. After choosing to forgive that person, she immediately felt a wash of warmth cover her, and her shoulder was completely healed.

E) Sometimes We Will Only Be Healed When We Obey

John 9:6-8 (NLT)
He spit on the ground, made mud with the saliva, and spread the mud over the blind man's eyes. He told him, "Go wash yourself in the pool of Siloam." So the man went and washed and came back seeing!

Can you imagine? Making a mud pie out of saliva and putting it into someone's eyes? A little unorthodox to say the least. This man had a choice. He could go and wash as Jesus told him to do, or he could get offended. I believe a lot of people in today's "church" get offended more often than just doing what God tells them to do. *"You want me to do what??"* they say, *"I don't think so. Do you know everything I do for this church? Do you know I sit on the elder's board? I'm above that kind of humbling behavior. You churches are all the same! I deserve more."* Their arguments go on and on. This man did something different. He humbled himself, put his pride aside, and did what Jesus told him to. As a result, the blind man was healed.

I've heard all kinds of stories over the years about people getting healed, just because they followed the directions that God gave them. Sometimes it's the act of forgiving someone. Other times it's changing the way you eat! Yes, that's practical but, guess what? God's a practical God and He knows how our bodies were meant to be treated.

One time we had a surgeon in a service who had been dealing with chronic pain for a long time. He brought an offering forward in a special service, after having resisted the urge to give previously. The moment he let go of the offering, the pain left him. I tell this story and I'm not trying to say that giving is the way to bring about physical healing. I'm just saying that if we live a life of doing what God asks us to do, we will always be in a place where we can be healed. There's another profound example of this in the Bible, and it's one of my favorite examples.

Luke 17:11-19 (NIV) Ten Healed of Leprosy

Now on his way to Jerusalem, Jesus traveled along the border between Samaria and Galilee. As he was going into a village, ten men who had leprosy met him. They stood at a distance and called out in a loud voice, "Jesus, Master, have pity on us!" When he saw them, he said, "Go, show yourselves to the priests." And as they went, they were cleansed. One of them, when he saw he was healed, came back, praising God in a loud voice. He threw himself at Jesus' feet and thanked him—and he was a Samaritan. Jesus asked, "Were not all ten cleansed? Where are the other nine? Was no one found to return and give praise to God except this foreigner?" Then he said to him, "Rise and go; your faith has made you well."

Notice it says, " . . . *as they went* . . ." they were cleansed. It means that once Jesus prayed for them and they started on their way, the disease of leprosy was no longer on them. There would be no more damage to their bodies from that point on. For they had to first "go" in faith before they were healed of this horrible disease. We need to start acting as if we are healed, too! It's through this action that we set the stage for our healing to manifest.

Let's dive further into this story! The Bible says there were ten lepers cleansed. The leprosy had been halted. But only one of the lepers returned to Jesus to thank Him! I'm sure the others were just as excited to be cleansed. And, for whatever reason, they still didn't feel the need to come back to Jesus and thank Him.

Notice that because the one was thankful, Jesus made him "well." Another word for well is "whole." To put it differently, the leprosy wasn't just stopped, but the body parts that he lost because of the disease were restored. He was made completely whole!

The others would still wear the scars of leprosy, but not this one. He was whole. How much more will God do for us when we stay in a place of gratitude and thankfulness. Thank him every day for your health. For what He's doing in your life—not only for what you can already see—but also for that which is still to come. Watch how your life starts becoming "whole."

F) Watch What You Say

Proverbs 18:21 (NKJV)
Death and life are in the power of the tongue, and those who love it will eat its fruit.

We spent a whole chapter on this, but it's so important to realize that we may receive sickness by either fear or by our own mouth. We can be so scared of getting cancer, we actually open a door for the devil to walk it right into our lives! Shut down fear! And watch your words. It's so easy to take ownership of things we should never be touching, just by speaking over our lives with certain words. *"My family all has diabetes. I'm bound to get it." "I have cancer." "I'm sick and tired."* Every time we open our mouths we get in agreement with either Satan's strategy to make us sick, or God's plan to heal us. It can't be both. It's one or the other. Instead of using the negative statements above, try these instead: *"My family has dealt with diabetes, but praise God I don't have to receive that." "I've been diagnosed with cancer, but praise God it's dead at the root and will have to manifest as healing."* Do you get the picture?

Don't get all weird with this and say *"Look where the dog didn't bite me,"* when you have a gaping hole in your arm. No! Faith doesn't deny reality, it just overrides it! You don't have to deny where you're at, but make sure that your words point to where you're going! You may be dealing with allergies, but your words should be declaring that it's just a season, and that healing is manifesting more and more in your life every day.

Be willing to fight the good fight of faith! I know that sometimes it can feel overwhelming. It's hard to have faith when you're puking over a toilet. I get it. That's why you need to surround yourself with people who can encourage you and help hold you up in your faith when you are too tired to fight yourself. There's power in agreement.

Also, always use wisdom. Don't go off medications just because you feel like you're healed. Get a doctor to check you out. If you're healed, the doctor will have to make adjustments. Medicine won't stop God from healing you. He is big enough to work alongside doctors, and guide you to when changes need to be made. Just be very careful to stay in touch with your doctor! If you are diabetic and praying for healing, keep on taking your meds until you are fully healed. It could be dangerous not to. Use wisdom, pray for clarity, and don't be scared of a doctor. God uses them all the time to help heal people. Our son Ashton, who was diagnosed with a severe allergy at only one year, was also diagnosed with a huge hole in the chamber wall of his heart. They wanted to do surgery in the very near future. Ralph and I would never think of taking a bet with our son's life. If surgery were needed, we would have okayed it. That said, we asked the doctors, *"How long can we wait until it's absolutely necessary to have the surgery?"* In other words, how long can you give us before we have no choice but to do surgery. They said our son had three years at the absolute maximum before he needed this particular surgery in order to save his life. Well, we took the time! We started praying over his heart and commanding the hole to close up. Three years later, we went into the Children's Heart Center to have his heart checked, in our doctors minds, to schedule the surgery.

Ashton was so sweet. He was singing at the top of his lungs in the waiting room. It wasn't just that he was singing, but *what* he was singing. "My little heart's got a great big love, a great big love for Jesus." Couldn't have declared it better myself!

The examination showed another medical miracle. The hole had completely closed up, which they said was impossible due to its size. Nothing is impossible for our God! The point I'm making is this: you don't have to fight against the medical profession. Work with them. Pray for favor with them. But use wisdom. The end goal is that you are healthy and whole. How you get there is not the main issue. It's getting there that's most important.

11

WHY AM I LIKE THIS?
DEALING WITH INIQUITIES

Romans 7:18-19 (NLT)

I want to do what is right, but I can't.
I want to do what is good, but I don't.
I don't want to do what is wrong, but I do it anyway.

About five years ago, I heard someone explain away their ungodly behavior with, *"Well, I was born this way!"* When I first heard them tell me that, I thought, *"What a lame excuse."* But the more I thought about it, the more I realized that there was a kernel of truth in it. Aren't we all born with a tendency to sin?

How many times have you heard someone blame a behavior on their heritage. If someone says, *"Oh, I'm Italian!"* or *"Oh, I'm Irish!"* we all know exactly what they mean. Certain traits and behaviors are passed down through cultures and families. In the same way, sin tendencies can also get passed down to us. We can all agree that our family has at least one issue: maybe it's addiction, anger, or even selfishness, that multiple people can struggle with.

It can be an incredibly frustrating thing to know you're acting out a sin tendency that you saw in your parents. Even though you love God with all your heart, you still can't seem to break out of it! Every time you think you've overcome it, that you're making progress, it comes right back! It's still holding you captive.

I knew there was more to the story. I just had to figure out what it was. Over the next nine months, God took me on an amazing journey of discovery. Thankfully, that journey led us to freedom.

Psalm 51:2-3 (NKJV)
Wash me thoroughly from my iniquity, And cleanse me from my sin. For I acknowledge my transgressions, And my sin is always before me.

For a long time, I had always assumed the words iniquity, sin, and transgression meant the same thing! That they were all basically talking about sin! What I also knew was that God is a very intentional God. Why would He use three different words to describe the same thing? There had to be more.

Well, there was! The more I looked, the more I found. Sin, iniquity, and transgression were not the same thing. They each have very specific meanings.

Sin – Missing the Mark
It was Paul who said, *"We all miss the mark."* We mess up and make mistakes when we don't intend to. Even though we try to walk on the straight and narrow, sometimes we stumble, fall, or get sidetracked. We call that sin.

Transgression – Intentionally Hurting God or Another
When you know what the right thing to do is, but you decide to do something else, you commit a transgression! We know we're not supposed to gossip, but we do it anyway. The news is just too juicy for us to give in to our better nature! We know we're supposed to forgive the person who hurt us, but we don't feel they deserve it, so we just don't do it.

Iniquity – A Sin Tendency

A sin tendency is a sin pattern that you haven't been able to overcome. It doesn't mean that you always act on it, but you struggle with it. Anger is a great example of a sin people struggle with. If you're quick to anger, it's easy to lash out at others. Through therapy and self-discipline, you can learn to control your anger—to a point! The same is true if you're an alcoholic. Even if you learn how to stay sober, once an addict, always an addict. The desire to drink does not go away, even if you learn how to manage it. Iniquity works in the same way. Whether you were born that way, or developed the habit as a response to an event or trauma, if you're still tempted, you haven't overcome it yet.

Growing up, I used to hear a lot about generational curses. Not totally knowing how they worked, where it was found in scripture or how to break them, the more I asked other mature Christians around me, the more I realized I wasn't the only one having trouble dealing with or understanding them.

I believe when most people refer to a generational curse they're talking about an iniquity. To put it a different way, a generational curse is a sin tendency that has been passed down generationally. We see examples of generational curses all the time: a family that struggles with generations of addiction, an illness that is passed down from one generation to another, a history of anger with multiple generations dealing with physical abuse. Every family's generational curse is different.

Psalm 51:5 (NKJV)

Behold, I was brought forth in iniquity, And in sin my mother conceived me.

In today's language, if we say a child was born in sin, it means that the child was born out of wedlock. That wasn't the case for David! His mother wasn't sinning when she gave birth to him. Rather, David was born *INTO* a sin tendency. In Psalm 51, he recognized there was some sin passed down to him.

What was true for David is true also for us. We are *all* born into a sin tendency. It is passed down generationally until we overcome it.

Exodus 20:5-6 (NKJV)

I, the Lord your God, am a jealous God, visiting the iniquity of the fathers upon the children to the third and fourth generations of those who hate Me, but showing mercy to thousands, to those who love Me and keep My commandments.

Each of us has iniquities and sin tendencies that have been passed down to us through our parents. So many of us are beating ourselves up because we haven't been able to overcome the sin in our lives. We feel shame, defeat, and condemnation. Even when we love God, we haven't been able to get set free!

Romans 7:15 (NLT)

I don't really understand myself, for I want to do what is right, but I don't do it. Instead, I do what I hate.

Let me be clear, there is never an excuse for sin. That said, one of the ways the Bible helps us overcome it is by teaching us why we do it.

Exodus 34:7 (NLT)

I lavish unfailing love to a thousand generations. I forgive iniquity, rebellion, and sin. But I do not excuse the guilty. I lay the sins of the parents upon their children and grandchildren; the entire family is affected—even children in the third and fourth generations.

The first part of this passage is great news! God will forgive all of our sins. At the same time, He still holds us accountable for our actions, even if it's a generational sin. In other words, God doesn't let us be the victim! By not allowing us to have an excuse, we can't play the *"poor me"* card. *"That's just not fair!"* you might say. *"How come I have to be held accountable for what my parents did?"*

Romans 7:18-23 (NLT)

And I know that nothing good lives in me, that is, in my sinful nature. I want to do what is right, but I can't. I want to do what is good, but I don't. I don't want to do what is wrong, but I do it anyway. But if I do what I don't want to do, I am not really the one doing wrong; it is sin living in me that does it. I have discovered this principle of life—that when I want to do what is right, I inevitably do what is wrong. I love God's law with all my heart. But there is another power within me that is at war with my mind. This power makes me a slave to the sin that is still within me.

It doesn't matter who you are, every human being was born with a sin nature. You don't have a problem with alcoholism, you have a problem with your sin nature. You don't have a problem with lying, you have a problem with your sin nature. Every one of the sins we commit can find its origin in our sin nature.

Without Christ, our sin nature is what controls our actions. Even though we can practice self-control and think rationally about our actions, our own willpower by itself is not enough to overcome our sin nature. You may be able to manage it for a while, but you will never fully overcome it. That's why, outside of Jesus Christ, it's hard to create lasting change in your life. Our sin nature, which we were all born with by default, and is a byproduct of growing up in a sinful world, controls us.

But there's good news!

Romans 7:24-25 (NLT)

Oh, what a miserable person I am! Who will free me from this life that is dominated by sin and death? Thank God! The answer is in Jesus Christ our Lord. So you see how it is: In my mind I really want to obey God's law, but because of my sinful nature I am a slave to sin.

Jesus is the answer! Many of us describe the experience of accepting Jesus into our lives as being "born again." Obviously, we can't physically go back into our mother's womb and be born again. What we are referring to is a spiritual birth.

John 3:6-7 (AMP)

That which is born of the flesh is flesh [the physical is merely physical], and that which is born of the Spirit is spirit. Do not be surprised that I have told you, 'You must be born again [reborn from above—spiritually transformed, renewed, sanctified].'

Jesus didn't come just to offer us salvation, He also came to give us a new nature. A nature that is no longer dominated by sin. It is through His grace that our broken-down and sinful spirit is exchanged for a *new spirit* with a *new nature*, and made whole in Christ. It's the difference between patching up an old house with paint and flooring or tearing it down and building it new from the ground up. God doesn't want us to use bandages to fix our issues. He wants to give us a whole new nature and a new shot at life.

Our Own Story

Early in our marriage, Ralph and I really struggled a lot. Part of our issues came from Ralph's anger problem. I never really noticed it when we were dating. However, once we were married, it was out in full view. As his wife, I didn't know how to help him with it. The fact that he wasn't angry towards me helped. But as his spouse, I didn't know how to help him or how to handle the anger. Years later, Ralph was inspired by a tape series a friend gave him about Walking in Love. He had a revelation that this anger to people was not God's best for him, and was blatantly sin. He had never seen it from that perspective before. It changed how he responded to situations, and for the most part, he was able to manage his anger. But every so often, someone would push his buttons in just the right way. When that happened, Ralph's anger came back in full force.

When I say my husband used to get mad, it wasn't just a *"hey, I'm mad"* kind of mad. It was an *"I'm mad and I want to kill that guy and his whole family"* kind of mad. When I first heard Ralph use the phrase *"I'll kill you if ..."* I didn't think he actually meant it.

Well, the summer after I started studying iniquity, I discovered just how literally Ralph meant it. At the time, we were going through an on-slaught of attacks. We were also being sued. Even though the law and case study was on our side, we kept losing every time we were in court. It didn't make any sense.

By the end of it, we had lost about half a million dollars in judge-ments and fees. Ouch! By this point, every single one of Ralph's buttons had gotten pushed, big time!! He wanted someone to die. The moment he started talking about how great it would be to hire a hit man, I knew he had a problem. Praise God he never went through with it, but still it was a problem.

> **1 John 3:15** (NLT)
> *Anyone who hates another brother or sister is really a murderer at heart. And you know that murderers don't have eternal life within them.*

One day, Ralph was sitting in his office pondering the truth of this verse. He was so broken inside! He knew he wasn't supposed to hate people as much as he did, but he couldn't help himself. Here he was, a pastor, and wanted to see people killed!

You see, he had learned how to *manage* his anger through hearing about what God's Word said about it, but he still wasn't *free* from it. Many people manage their addictions, but are not free. There's always the lingering de-sire to go back to the old way. That's not God's freedom! As he sat there in his office by himself, Ralph cried out to God for help.

A couple of days later, our son Connor told us he had been doing a genealogy study of the Hoehne family. Not knowing really anything about our legal troubles, or what Ralph had been wrestling with, Connor had discovered that a few generations ago, a number of Ralph's fam-ily members had been hit men for the German and Swiss governments! *"Whaaat???? Are you kidding me?"* We also found out that a few more of his relatives were enforcers that the Italian mafia used to pay to take out crooked judges and government officials. It took us a couple days to connect all the dots. But once we did, we realized where the root of all this anger was! This is why Ralph was so outraged all the time and felt the urge to see people killed!

God had finally given us the key: Combining the genealogy knowledge with the revelation God had given us about iniquities was it! Now, Ralph's next step was to walk through the door.

Isaiah 53:5-6 (NKJV)

But He was wounded for our transgressions, He was bruised for our iniquities; The chastisement for our peace was upon Him, And by His stripes we are healed. All we like sheep have gone astray; We have turned, every one, to his own way; And the LORD has laid on Him the iniquity of us all.

Have you ever had a bruise? For some reason, I bruise very easily. I can end up with a big bruise all over my leg and have no idea how it got there. The interesting thing about bruises is that you can't feel them unless something touches or rubs up against it. If I had a bruise on my shoulder that you couldn't see, I wouldn't feel it. But if you came up and touched my shoulder as you said hello, I would jump!! Touching a bruise can cause instant pain that wasn't there the moment before. Sometimes, you don't even know you have a bruise until it gets touched. Iniquities are discovered in the exact same way. They're a bruise!

You don't always know they're there until you accidentally stumble upon one. You don't know you have an addictive personality until you take your first drink of alcohol. Or maybe you know you do, but the pain doesn't come until it's hit in just the right way. Ralph didn't realize how angry he was until he was in a storm.

The revelation Ralph received that day was that Jesus really did pray the price for his anger. He took all of our iniquity and nailed it to the cross for us. He took it so we wouldn't have to be stuck with it. In the same way Christ's death brought healing into our physical bodies, so did it bring freedom from our iniquities. Some have argued with me that you are automatically set free from iniquity when you become born again. But I would have to disagree. Healing is also mentioned in Isaiah 53. But haven't you known or even been a Christian who is fully born again but dealing with sickness? Until you get the revelation on healing, you're not able to receive it.

Finding Freedom

Ephesians 2:1-3,8 (NLT)
God saved you by his grace when you believed. And you can't take credit for this; it is a gift from God.

The first step towards overcoming an iniquity is to *believe* that Christ has set you free. Your freedom, just the same as your healing, is not something you can earn. Instead, it's about having a revelation on it so you can receive it by faith. Everything in the kingdom of God is received by faith. Even salvation! We have to believe before we can receive. It's the same with iniquity.

"*So, how do I receive it?*" Ralph said a simple prayer while he sat in his office meditating on the verse God gave him. He said, "*Father, I now see you paid the price for iniquity. You took care of it all on the cross. In Jesus name I now break off this iniquity and receive your full payment and healing.*" Then he waited.

Ralph told me later that, as he prayed, he felt nothing, and didn't even know if it actually worked. A few days later we were at home watching an action movie together. Normally, Ralph would mutter things like "get 'em" while throwing pretend punches, etc. Any of you guys do that? I always find it *quite* interesting. Well, this time, things were different. As we watched two characters go at it, instead of giving me his normal reaction, Ralph felt compassion for the guy who was losing! Deep compassion.

As he spoke, I looked at him and asked, "*Who are you and what have you done with my husband?*" An alien must have invaded earth and taken over his body. I was sure of it! Eventually, Ralph told me what had happened, how he had prayed in his office, and how free he felt.

As we shared this story with our boys, they all kind of agreed that they had dealt with the same thing their father had! As I listened to them, I kind of laughed. All the many times I had put them in a hotel room together and joked that they were about to kill each other, I had no idea how true it was! After they were done, we showed them how to pray as Ralph had. It was their first step towards walking the journey to freedom as well.

Ralph and I weren't able to break the chain of iniquity before our children were born, but at least we were now able to walk our kids into freedom. It is a blessing we believe will last for generations. For once iniquity is broken, as long as you don't pick it up again, the generations that follow behind you will not have to deal with it. Praise God for that!

John 8:36 (AMP)
So if the Son liberates you [makes you free men], then you are really and unquestionably free.

Definition of FREE: set at liberty: from the dominion of sin

There's a difference between controlling or managing your sin, and being free. AA is an incredible organization that has helped thousands of people deal with alcoholism. However, it requires addicts to go to meetings for years and years, if not for the rest of their lives, so they can *manage* the addiction and avoid falling back into it. Even though it's a lot of work, going to meetings is a much better option than a life of alcoholism. At the same time, it's not true freedom.

You see, when Christ sets you free you are truly free indeed. I still remember when we told Ralph's story in a series at our church. Imagine having your pastor confess from the platform that he had felt like killing people! It was a *quiet* crowd that Sunday morning, to say the least. We always stand at the door and say goodbye to people. I watched many people try to avoid Ralph like the plague! It was pretty funny. At the same time, it was totally worth it. We were able to see so many people catch the revelation. One man had been using chewing tobacco for 30 years but just couldn't quit. It was a habit his father had started him on. The revelation hit him; he prayed and was freed that day! For others it was fear. One woman realized that she had a fear of being home alone at night. Once she realized her mother was the same, she broke it and has been free ever since. From addictions and fears to people wrestling with insecurities and low self-esteem, once they realized that God could break them out of bondage, they were set free.

Emotional Iniquities

As we shared this message with our church, one area we noticed a lot of people struggling with was overcoming emotional iniquities. It's not just the physical tendencies such as abuse or addiction that get passed down generationally. Emotional wounds, pain, and unforgiveness get passed down as well.

How many people do you see walking around with a victim mentality about something that happened to their ancestors? Even though the trauma took place generations before, they still carry it around with them today. Other people just feel like a victim. They walk around wounded, but have no idea why!

A family we know had a mother who had been sexually assaulted by a family member while she was growing up. She went on to have children of her own, and eventually accepted Christ and chose to forgive this person. God did a huge restoration in her life and in fact restored the relationship with this person as well, who later asked for forgiveness.

But the key point here is that the daughter had been dealing with night terrors and physical ailments from a very young age, and they had no idea why. As we brought this teaching of iniquity to our church, this mom was sharing her concern with me. Something in my spirit said it had to do with iniquity. That somehow the trauma the mom had felt and experienced was being passed to the daughter! Now let me tell you, this was too crazy for even me to grasp in my natural mind. It still is! But I felt the Holy Spirit leading me in this so strongly. I shared with the mom, she agreed and we prayed.

From that point on those night terrors and physical ailments broke! This is a family who had prayed the word of God over their daughter, and spoke healing and peace. The little girl knew more scripture than most adults, but still she hadn't found freedom. Until now. Years later she is still completely free.

A few years ago, I ran into an old friend who had confided in me about problems she was having with her young daughter. She was dealing with depression, was constantly withdrawn, and for some strange reason, kept attracting unwanted "sexual attention" from men and boys of all ages. My friend was at a loss. She didn't think her daughter acted or looked promiscuous, yet men kept treating her as if she were.

My friend had put her in counseling and enforced strict boundaries around her. Even so, they still couldn't figure it out. Her daughter hadn't been abused. Yet there was a cloud that hung around her. The parents were deeply concerned that someone would eventually take advantage of her.

The more my friend told me, the more stumped I was. I had known her and her family for most of my life. The more I prayed about it, the more I felt the spirit telling me it was iniquity. After asking a few more questions about my friend's family history, I found out that her mother, her daughter's grandmother, had been sexually abused as a child. Like her granddaughter, she also dealt with depression, and was never able to get over the trauma she endured.

Wow! Once again, the passing of a trauma. I shared with my friend what God had shown me about iniquities. Once she got home, she shared it with her husband and daughter and immediately prayed over her. There wasn't an immediate change as in the earlier story, but it started the healing process. Over the next year, my friend's daughter started to find joy and freedom again. When I saw my friend a year later, she was thrilled that she was finally able to help her daughter begin the process of becoming healthy and whole.

I believe so many people suffocate under the weight of depression and trauma that is inherited through iniquity.

True Freedom is Ours

Titus 2:14 (AMP)
Who gave Himself on our behalf that He might redeem us (purchase our freedom) from all iniquity and purify for Himself a people [to be peculiarly His own, people who are] eager and enthusiastic about [living a life that is good and filled with] beneficial deeds.

Purchase us from *all* iniquity. What good news. God's plan for us was never to live under the weight of our iniquity. Jesus paid for all of it, so we could be enthusiastic about life! Now, we no longer have to be controlled by those things.

Psalm 119:132-133 (NKJV)
Look upon me and be merciful to me, As Your custom is toward those who love Your name. Direct my steps by Your word, And let no iniquity have dominion over me.

No matter what story you come from, or the situation you were raised in, *the God IN you is greater than the story you came from!* Addictions don't have to run in your family any more. Anger, fear, hate and perversions can end today! YOU can be the one that changes the story of your family for generations to come.

John 8:36 (AMP)
So if the Son liberates you [makes you free men], then you are really and unquestionably free.

Once you obtain freedom in Christ, you can be sure that you are indeed free. If you want to see that freedom manifest in every area of your life, you have to walk that freedom out. The things that came at you in the past, will of course, come again. I guarantee it.

Ralph always described it this way. When a negative thought entered his mind, it would grab him and sink its nails in. No matter how hard he tried, He wouldn't be able to shake it. After asking God to set him free, the thoughts would still come at him. This time, however, with God's freedom, the thoughts would slide right off of him.

I explained earlier how thoughts, imaginations, and strongholds work. When a negative thought or feeling comes at you, if you don't recognize that Jesus has set you free, and declare it over that thought, you will be tempted to entertain it again. When you entertain it long enough, it can once again become a stronghold in your life.

Never forget, that once you are free, thoughts do *not* have dominion over your life anymore. You *are* free, and by the power of the Holy Spirit, and under the authority of what Jesus Christ did for you on the cross, you don't need to submit yourself to it anymore. But it's your choice. Please choose freedom! It's worth the fight.

For more teaching about how to overcome iniquities, check out our series "Why Am I Like This?"

12

LOVE AND FORGIVENESS

"Love and Serve People to Life."

That's our mission statement at The Source Church, which Ralph and I planted nine years ago, and still pastor today. It seems like such a simple idea, but it's been a 20-year journey finding out what it really means to love and serve others. If anyone has ever *"stepped on your blue suede shoes,"* or left you hurt or offended, you'll know that love is not the first reaction you would have towards that person. Anger, frustration and a few choice words are probably more accurate in describing how you would feel!

I've seen it over and over again as a pastor. Love can change the hardest of hearts. It can break down the walls that often divide us along racial, socioeconomic, and cultural lines. We've seen it happen hundreds of times in our church. At the end of the day, people just want to be loved! It doesn't matter what walk of life they come from. Love is a bridge that, if crossed, can lead you into a life of freedom and wholeness. It can heal the most wounded parts of your soul. Not only for you, but also for the person that may have hurt you.

"That's most unfortunate"

"That's most unfortunate." That might not seem like a very angry response to a negative situation. In fact, if someone really pushed your buttons, I could guess your response would probably sound more aggressive than that. But for my dad, Ted Bradford, that was literally the worst thing I ever heard him say about *anyone*. When we heard that statement, we knew that, whatever had happened, must have been pretty bad! My mom and dad, Ted and Rheta Bradford, were and are exceptional people.

Even though my dad went to be with Jesus twelve years ago, he set a very high standard for how to walk in love. My parents raised me to always love others easily and forgive people quickly. Ralph did not have the same teaching. He had a justice side to him that had a zero tolerance approach towards being taken advantage of. With that worldview, he often became angry and felt very justified in doing so. His reasoning was that if God were a just God, wouldn't He want Ralph to carry out His justice? At the time, he thought he was helping God whenever he stuck it to someone who deserved it. What he didn't know at the time was that God has two things he never wants us to take from Him: His glory and His vengeance.

Romans 12:19 (AMP)

Beloved, never avenge yourselves, but leave the way open for God's wrath [and His judicial righteousness]; for it is written [in Scripture], "Vengeance is Mine, I will repay," says the Lord.

Twenty years ago, a friend handed Ralph a series of cassette tapes called *The Love Walk*. Those six tapes changed our lives forever! Without exaggeration, Ralph must have listened to that series sixty to eighty different times. Every time he replayed it, its truths went deeper and deeper into his spirit. Even though I grew up in a loving and forgiving home, I never heard anyone teach on the art of loving others!

Learning to love and understanding how dangerous it was to harbor offense in his heart transformed Ralph and changed the way he responded to people around him. Slowly but surely, he learned to control his anger. He no longer felt the burden and weight of having to harbor grudges or carry the load of "making people pay." He enjoyed life so much more. We even saw an improvement in our marriage. Love won!

1 Corinthians 13:13 (NLT)
Three things will last forever—faith, hope, and love—and the greatest of these is love.

I hope by this point in the book, I've been able to instill faith and hope in you. Don't get me wrong! Faith and hope are great! But love is the greatest. I've left the best for last!

It's vital that every Christian has a comprehensive understanding about what love is all about. In church we love to hear about how much God loves us, but we often don't pay the same amount of attention to God's commandment to love others. If you want the absolute key to success, every time, I'll tell you what it is: Love.

1 Corinthians 13:8 (NKJV)
Love never fails.

If you want your life to count, then you need to learn to love.

1 Corinthians 13:2 (NLT)
If I had the gift of prophecy, and if I understood all of God's secret plans and possessed all knowledge, and if I had such faith that I could move mountains, but didn't love others, I would be nothing.

We are capable of doing a lot of great things in life. Both for God and ourselves. We can see miracles, counsel kings and world leaders, build a business empire that gives millions to worthy causes! But even so, the Bible says if we don't love others it's all for nothing. Love is the acid test for everything! You won't be judged by how great your ministry was or how successful you were. It will be how well you loved. How well you forgave others after they hurt or offended you! If you can't love, you'll be disqualified.

Have you ever prepared for a race or competition? Maybe it was a marathon, or a promotion, or a contest of some kind. Imagine having one year to prepare for a business presentation. It's for an account you've been working towards your whole career. And *everything*, all your finances, time, and effort are on the line. Imagine finding out on the day you're scheduled to present that you have been disqualified. They tell you that a few forms you didn't know about should have been submitted weeks ago in order to be eligible for the opportunity. Imagine how you would feel?! All your work for the last year, wasted. You're left broken and defeated.

That's where our Christian walk with God is at when we don't walk in love. Yes, as Christians, we work for our reward in heaven. But all our sacrifice will be in vain if we haven't learned to love. We will be disqualified. All of it, for nothing. Loving others is that important.

Matthew 22:36-40 (NLT)

"Teacher, which is the most important commandment in the law of Moses?" Jesus replied, "'You must love the Lord your God with all your heart, all your soul, and all your mind.' This is the first and greatest commandment. A second is equally important: 'Love your neighbor as yourself.' The entire law and all the demands of the prophets are based on these two commandments."

Love is the bedrock of the two greatest commandments. When you love others, you won't sin against them. This means you won't steal from them, kill them or break any other laws that were given to Moses. It fulfills them all.

Notice that, for as much as we know loving God is vital in our Christian walk, Jesus said that loving others is just as important! Not just loving others, but loving them as you love yourself. Wow! That puts an unexpected twist on this love thing. In other words, we need to be loving and treating people *as we* want to be treated and loved. Do *you* want to be gossiped about? Do *you* want nasty things said to you or about you? Do *you* want to be ignored and judged by how you dress or speak? Do *you* want to be judged and remembered by your greatest mistakes? Or by the color of your skin or your cultural background? Maybe some of you like pain and being victimized, but I can safely say that most people would say a big *NO* to all those questions. If *we* don't want that kind of treatment ourselves, we are not to treat others that way either. Remember, what you sow, you will reap!

Matthew 7:2 (NLT)
For you will be treated as you treat others. The standard you use in judging is the standard by which you will be judged.

God has set a pretty high standard that doesn't really leave room for us to stay offended by or angry with others.

Love is a decision. It's not always a feeling. We don't have to like someone to love someone. Now, many times the two will go hand in hand, but other times they won't! Just because you don't like someone doesn't mean that love isn't required.

Romans 13:8 (NLT)
Owe nothing to anyone—except for your obligation to love one another. If you love your neighbor, you will fulfill the requirements of God's law.

The Safety of Love
Scripture tell us, if we love others, we fulfill God's requirements! Love cancels out all the punishments or judgments that would come to us from disobeying the law.

Never forget that satan is your enemy. He will take every opportunity he gets to try and trip you up. He wants you to break God's commandments. Just a little jealousy here, and a little white lie there. But if you walk in love, it shuts him down! Love *protects* us from the desire to commit sins against others, just as love towards God *protects* us from the desire to sin against God! Love trumps it all. When you learn to walk in love towards both God and others, the enemy will have a much harder time finding a foothold in your life.

What Does Love Look Like

John 15:12 (NLT)

This is my commandment: Love each other in the same way I have loved you.

Love the same way God loved us. How did Jesus love us? Unconditionally. Without waiting for us to get everything right, He loved us with compassion. He saw people's hurts and fears. He hung out with the outcasts of society. He spread hope and love to everyone around him and never judged.

You may not be able to control how other people feel about you, or treat you. You may not even be able to get others to forgive you when you mess up! But the thing you can control is how you respond and treat *them.* Love them, not when they have it all together, but when they are far from getting it together. Just as God loved us in our sin, so must we love others in their mess and dysfunction as well!

So, now that we know we are called to love others, let's exam what that love is supposed to look like.

1 Corinthians 13:4-7 (NIRV)

Love is patient. Love is kind. It does not want what belongs to others. It does not brag. It is not proud. It does not dishonor other people. It does not look out for its own interests. It does not easily become angry. It does not keep track of other people's wrongs. Love is not happy with evil. But it is full of joy when the truth is spoken. It always protects. It always trusts. It always hopes. It never gives up.

We could teach a hundred series and write dozens of books about this alone. It's a high standard for sure. But if how you're treating others doesn't resemble this list, then you have some work to do! If loving and forgiving people is hard for you, may I suggest printing off these verses in 1 Corinthians and meditating on them daily. Let God reframe your thought life with the word and paint a new picture of how He wants you to live in love.

How Do We Love?

Earlier, I told you about my father, and how he lived an incredible life full of love and forgiveness. Even though I never knew him any other way, before he died, he told me he wasn't always like that. He had *chosen* to cover people with love. He had chosen to cover their sins and mistakes with love.

He told me he realized that, when you love someone who hates you, *you* win!! That small change in the way he approached life empowered him to literally impact thousands of people's lives in a positive way. Even though he never pastored, wrote a book or preached from a platform, his life impacted people everywhere he went. People may not always remember what you say, but they *will* remember how you made them feel. To this day, people still tell me stories about how my dad, decades ago, helped change their lives.

What does it look like when someone has hurt you beyond comprehension? When you have every right to be hurt and wounded?

Matthew 5:44-48 (NLT)

But I say, love your enemies! Pray for those who persecute you! In that way, you will be acting as true children of your Father in heaven. For he gives his sunlight to both the evil and the good, and he sends rain on the just and the unjust alike. If you love only those who love you, what reward is there for that? Even corrupt tax collectors do that much. If you are kind only to your friends, how are you different from anyone else? Even pagans do that. But you are to be perfect, even as your Father in heaven is perfect.

We start the journey of loving others when we pray for them. Not only when they are nice to us, but especially when they attack us. Now, if you're like Ralph, when you first start praying for someone, you might be tempted to pray something like " . . . please let them get hit by a truck!" But, I don't think that's what God meant when He said pray for others. We should pray for their well-being. That God might move on their hearts. That He might reveal Himself to them. Then the hardest prayer of all; that He might bless them.

It could take you awhile to get there, but that's okay! Each time you pray for them, it will deflate the balloon of hurt and anger a little more. And eventually, no matter how badly they hurt you, you'll be full of so much love that you'll pray God's blessings and protection over them. The hurt that once held you captive will be replaced with compassion and freedom.

I have a couple of friends who were abused sexually by a parent, for many, many years. Both of them had to make the tough choice to forgive, and pray for their abusers. I asked each of them about their experience. They explained that, *"At first, it was hard, but eventually I got to the point where I only wanted the best for him!"* It was through love they went from hating the people who hurt them to wanting to protect them.

Of course, it took a lot of time for them to rebuild trust. They also didn't stay in the abusive situations. But, by praying for their abuser, they were all able to work through the suffering they had endured. Love, forgiveness and the prayer that went up for those abusive parents changed the situation! In both cases the parents eventually asked forgiveness and restored relationship to them. You see, love didn't make them weak, it actually made them strong. It brought healing and restoration.

1 John 4:7-8 (AMP)

Beloved, let us [unselfishly] love and seek the best for one another, for love is from God; and everyone who loves [others] is born of God and knows God [through personal experience]. The one who does not love has not become acquainted with God [does not and never did know Him], for God is love. [He is the originator of love, and it is an enduring attribute of His nature.]

God is not only the source of the love we have for others, but the act of loving others itself helps us know God better! It's the evidence that His Spirit lives in us. That we are getting to know His heart.

I also think loving others gives us a window into the inner heart of God–how He feels when He chooses to love us. It can remind us of all the times we turned our back on Him. Yet, even when we rejected Him, He still loved us!

This verse also implies that if we're not walking in love, we probably don't know God. Unfortunately, I've met whole churches and congregations that must not know God. They feel it's their job to judge people and put them down. We wonder why people aren't running to join the "club" of Christianity! I wouldn't sign up for that either.

I believe that every person in our life whom has ever hurt or offended us, was a test to see if God truly is in us or not. Just a little insight for you. If you don't pass the test, you'll have to take the course again and try again. Just as with school, if you fail the exam you'll need to redo it 'til you get it right.

As I mentioned earlier, the mission statement at our church is "Love and Serve People to Life." We believe that the fastest way to see God's vision for a person's life to come to fruition is to love and serve them. We've seen it over and over. Love always wins! As a church we have become a place where the first thing people say when they visit is how much they feel the love in the room.

A few years ago I was praying for God to expand our reach to the hurting. A dangerous prayer for sure, but I meant it. At the time, I was doing a lot of traveling. It didn't matter what flight I was on, I felt as if I were always getting seated by "interesting" people. A person scared of flying, or another with a story a mile long that they "had" to share. I remember one flight that was definitely a final exam experience for me.

While waiting at the gate, I noticed a woman, who was probably in her 40's, making quite a scene. Even though she was a middle-aged woman, she was dressed like a 15 year old boy, and wore headphones turned up so loud that everyone sitting around her could hear. She was also doing a live air guitar imitation! Right in the middle of the airport, she rocked out like there was no tomorrow!

It was quite a sight! I, including every other person at the gate, was hoping I wouldn't be the person sitting next to her. As I walked on the plane, I had hope. The flight wasn't full. This airline allows you to choose your own seat, so I chose a seat in the far back corner.

The very last person to board was this woman. I tentatively watched her as she made her way down the aisle. Passing rows of empty seats. My first reaction was, *"please don't let her sit by me!"* But God very quickly spoke to me: *"Do you want me to trust you with hurting people or not?"* I knew this was a chance to show God I was serious about what I had prayed for. So, in my heart I told God, *"OK God. Bring it on. Bring her to me and I'll love her like she's never been loved before".* Well, you guessed it. She passed at least twenty to thirty empty seats on the way to the seat next to me.

Almost immediately, I could see she was higher than a kite. She also wasted no time adding alcohol to the mix; singing away, having a grand old time with herself.

As the plane began to take off, she freaked out. She grabbed my arm and started having a panic attack. It was obvious she was afraid of flying! I found out that's why she had taken drugs, as a means of calming her nerves. She also told me she was on her way to visit her daughter whom she had not seen in over a year.

About halfway into the flight, someone close to us (who wasn't Ralph or myself - just saying) passed gas. Immediately, the woman next to us yelled at the *top* of her lungs, *"Who farted???? That's disgusting!!! Who did it? Oh my goodness who did it???"* She went on and on.

Everyone on the plane could hear her. We were all mortified. Still, that wasn't enough. Whoever had indeed done it, had not learned their lesson! About 20 minutes later, they did it again! And yes, her response was the same. Many more things happened on that flight, including her spilling a whole bottle of alcohol on my lap, as well as having to defuse angry passengers and flight attendants.

The only person who kept their cool was myself. Why? Because I had chosen love. Love protected me and kept me safe. Loving her as a choice gave me a different perspective and attitude, which produced a different emotion in me. Peace and compassion, instead of hate and frustration. At the end of that flight, as we were landing, she looked at me and asked how in the world I could have been so nice to her. How everyone else on the plane was hating her yet I had shown her nothing but kindness. I was able to share that I was showing her the same love that God had for her. It was my privilege to be able to do it. You see, love doesn't just affect the other person, it also changes us.

This kind of love pours out of our lives when we have a revelation of how great God's love for us is.

Ephesians 3:18 (NLT)
And may you have the power to understand, as all God's people should, how wide, how long, how high, and how deep his love is.

The security that comes from knowing there is a God who loves us un-conditionally, is what allows us to pour love out to others. You can't write a check from an account that's empty. You'll never be able to love others unless our love tank is filled by the love of God. Take the time to under-stand and receive the full love that God has for you. Study and meditate on how great His love for you is. How great a price He paid to forgive you and give you life.

When you realize how much God loves you and that you are cared for, no matter what others may say about you or do to you, you can love them in spite of it all. We don't love others in response to how they treat us, but in response to the love that the Father has poured out for us.

Your self worth and value is no longer based on how people treat you or what they say to you. If it is wrapped up in the love that God gives you; you're no longer threatened by those who hate you, ignore you, or treat you like they are better than you! It releases you to love those people who have not yet experienced the amazing love that our heavenly Father has to offer.

Colossians 3:12-15 (NLT)

Since God chose you to be the holy people he loves, you must clothe yourselves with tenderhearted mercy, kindness, humility, gentleness, and patience. Make allowance for each other's faults, and forgive anyone who offends you. Remember, the Lord forgave you, so you must forgive others. Above all, clothe yourselves with love, which binds us all together in perfect harmony. And let the peace that comes from Christ rule in your hearts. For as members of one body you are called to live in peace. And always be thankful.

This is a powerful scripture that shows us what love and forgiveness looks like. Notice that we have to clothe ourselves. I don't know about you, but no one magically clothes me in the morning when I wake up. And unless you have a disability or a physical challenge, it's probably the same for you. When I get up in the morning, I must clothe myself. It's the same with love and forgiveness. It's not automatically there! We must choose to put it on each and every day. We have to be intentional about it, *choosing* it every day.

Early on in our marriage, Ralph and I had a group of 20 people over to our home for dinner. It didn't take long for one couple, who had been married for a few years, to start sarcastically jabbing at each other. After the first one would say something, the other spouse would laugh and throw another jab back. It didn't stop there though. They continued to throw jab after jab after jab. Each comment getting more vicious than the last.

The room got tense very quickly. Before too long, people started leaving. Clearly, this couple had some major issues they were masking using humor and sarcasm. Well, I guarantee you that no one was really laughing. Them included. I am not a fan of sarcasm. It's just an easy way to hurt people with humor as an excuse. I don't believe that's God's heart at all.

As I listened to them go back and forth, I couldn't help but think, if one of them chose to respond in love instead of pain, the whole night could have gone differently. If one of them had chosen love, their marriage might of had a chance. But with both wanting their own way, their marriage was doomed.

It only takes *one* to release the supernatural force into a situation, that comes when we operate with love. You may be hurting as much as the other person, but when you choose love, it can totally change the dynamics of a situation.

I am so grateful that I chose love in my marriage. Many things have happened over the years, and many hurtful things have been said. But our marriage stands today because very early on, I chose love and forgiveness. For love never fails! Walking in love will free you from the weight of the hurt and offenses. Each offense you hold onto is like placing a rock in a backpack that you're carrying. One or two rocks may not feel very heavy, but a lifetime of those rocks will soon incapacitate you and leave you emotionally crippled. Love and forgiveness is what we call taking those rocks out of your backpack and leaving them on the side of the road. They free you.

Forgiveness

On a fall day, about 10 years before I was born, my mom and dad were raising two little boys while also expecting their first daughter, very shortly after. Life was good, and all was well. Until one fateful morning. In a moment, their entire life changed. While playing outside, my two year old brother Ronnie got startled and ran into the street and out in front of an oil truck that their neighbor was driving. He didn't see him, and tragically, Ronnie was hit and killed.

While my parents were at the hospital waiting to see if the doctors could revive Ronnie, the man who hit him was also there, pacing in the waiting room, talking about his own little boy.

My mom admitted how mad she was that he still had his little boy while she had just lost hers. I personally cannot begin to imagine the pain of losing a child, but I know that it's unlike any grief you can experience. It's totally reasonable she had feelings of anger and resentment. Later that same night, in the midst of all that pain, God spoke to both my parents, asking them to forgive the driver. Right away, my dad called the man and told him they held nothing against him. They knew it was an accident.

My mom told me years later that, after my father and her forgave the man, it was like a tangible heavy weight lifted off her back. Even though she was still grieving, the anger was gone. Through that experience, they realized they had not only been carrying the weight of grief, but the weight of unforgiveness as well. God knew there was no need for them carry both. In asking them to forgive, He brought them freedom.

How many of us are carrying a load we were never meant to carry? Forgiveness goes hand in hand with the love walk. In the same way not loving disqualifies you, not forgiving someone is like drinking poison, while hoping that the same poison will hurt the other person! Forgiveness is for *our* sake, just as much as it is for the other person.

Mark 11:25-26 (AMP)

Whenever you stand praying, if you have anything against anyone, forgive him [drop the issue, let it go], so that your Father who is in heaven will also forgive you your transgressions and wrongdoings [against Him and others]. ["But if you do not forgive, neither will your Father in heaven forgive your transgressions."]

*Whenever you pray...*In other words, if we want a clear line of communication with God; to know He hears our prayers, we need to *first* forgive others. Wow! There's no room for us to hold onto grudges and still live a life with God. The Bible clearly states, if you don't forgive others, He won't forgive you!

Matthew 6:15 (NLT)

But if you refuse to forgive others, your Father will not forgive your sins.

Dictionary: Forgive

To excuse for a fault or an offense; pardon
To renounce anger or resentment against
To absolve from payment of (a debt, for example)

I love the third definition. Forgiveness means that I do not have to walk out the full payment of my sins. That God can come into any situation and help bring favor even though I deserved to be punished. He removes the penalty for us. Even though there still might be physical consequences to our actions, God's grace comes in to rewrite your story in a beautiful new way. Without forgiveness, there is no chance for a rewrite! The full consequence of our sins and actions will come down on us.

If you want God's forgiveness in your life, you have to start by forgiving others. It breaks my heart when I hear people say they'll never forgive someone for something they did. They don't get it! By living in unforgiveness, they are putting a cancerous tumor into their spiritual life.

Again, it's not about the other person as much as it's about you! It's not about their guilt or innocence. Even Jesus forgave when they were guilty. In John 8, Jesus came across a woman who was caught in the act of adultery, who was about to be stoned. She was guilty! She didn't deny her sins, and Jesus didn't try to argue that she was innocent. She was in fact guilty. But He forgave her anyway.

John 8:10-11 (NLT)
Then Jesus stood up again and said to the woman, "Where are your accusers? Didn't even one of them condemn you?" "No, Lord," she said. And Jesus said, "Neither do I. Go and sin no more."

She didn't even ask for forgiveness, but still He gave it to her. Too many people get caught up in waiting to forgive until the other person apologizes and asks for it. The truth is, they may *never* come to you. All the while, you'll be left to carry the pain of it. *"Well,"* you might say. *"I'll forgive but I'll never forget!"*

Jeremiah 31:34(NLT)
"And I will forgive their wickedness, and I will never again remember their sins."

Remember: *zakar*
to cause to remember, remind
to mention
to record

If we are going to do this God's way, we need to "forget" when we forgive. Now, obviously we don't have the ability to wipe it from our memory, but we do have the ability to not hold it against them anymore. To not bring it up over and over or use it as a means of striking them. I am so grateful that God has not brought up my sins over and over again.

Psalm 103:12 (NLT)
He has removed our sins as far from us as the east is from the west.

God won't use our sin against us, because it's no longer between us. He has forgiven it and removed it. The more we allow unforgiveness into our lives, the more unforgiven sin creates a chasm between you and God. It can also actually cause sickness in our physical bodies! Forgiveness cleans that out and fully restores our relationship with our heavenly Father.
"But they keep doing it to me over and over again!"

Matthew 18:21-22 (NLT)
Then Peter came to him and asked, "Lord, how often should I forgive someone who sins against me? Seven times?" "No, not seven times," Jesus replied, "but seventy times seven!"

Some people just can't seem to get it right! They keep doing the same things over and over again. But then again, maybe it's you or I who are having trouble in an area, and need forgiveness over and over again.

I want to clarify something important. If you are in an abusive situation or are in danger of being physically harmed, you need to remove yourself from your situation! If someone is hurting your child, forgive them, but get the child to a safe place. If someone has stolen millions of dollars from you, forgive them, but fire them! Trust and forgiveness are two different things. Forgiveness is something that can happen in a moment, but trust is rebuilt over time. Sometimes, out of naiveness, we open the door for someone to sin against us over and over again. That's not what this Matthew 18 is talking about! Use wisdom and protect yourself. What it *is* talking about is the condition of your heart. We all make mistakes, and we all need to keep forgiving others of their mistakes as well.

Getting to The Bottom of Things

A number of years ago I was at the local Christian bookstore, and ran into a lady I had known at a previous church I had attended. Even though we were more acquaintances than friends, I always thought we had gotten along well. I was genuinely glad to see her! Our conversation, though, was quite a wake up call. After saying hello, she turned towards me. And with a big smile on her face, said, *"Wow! What a coincidence I meet you while we're in the aisle for books on forgiveness! That is so amazing!"* I was shocked and not quite sure how to respond.

I told her I was a little confused. Had I done something that hurt her? She said, *"yes!"* In fact, she said she had been carrying around my name in her Bible for 2 1/2 years, praying daily for the strength to forgive me. She told me it had absolutely consumed and tormented her!

I still didn't completely know how to respond. I hadn't seen her in over two years, and still had no Idea what I did to offend her. So I asked. She told me that, when we were at the same church, she had felt so rejected by me, because I didn't like her and found her area of ministry unimportant. I still had no idea where this had come from! I had always felt she was a great woman of God and had done a great job serving in the church.

It all came down to the fact that she had asked me to be her assistant in an area of ministry. I had prayed about it, but didn't feel released to do it. I thought it was a great project, but didn't feel as if I were the right fit for it. But she read so much more into it. Every time I only waved in the hall at her, she thought I was avoiding her. Every event I didn't show up to was my dislike of her ideas. She couldn't have been more wrong! But that's how the enemy works. He twists the truth in order to cause strife. He is the author of lies, and without knowing it, we can soak them up without filtering them out.

I can tell you confidently that we set the record straight that day. A simple misunderstanding that could have been cleared up with a fifteen-minute conversation, caused this woman two years of agonizing grief. Her unforgiveness nearly destroyed her even though it didn't hurt me in the least. But that's the price we pay when we choose not to forgive. You see, unforgiveness is like drinking poison yourself, and hoping it will kill the other person.

How to Handle Offense

When you've been hurt or offended, forgive and move on if you can. If you tried to "talk out" every single thing others did to you, it would quickly get old. It wouldn't take long before every time you walked into a room, people would scatter. No one likes to hear about their list of failures.

For the other times you can't just move past what someone did, you should confront them in love. But test your heart before you confront them. Will it hurt a little if you confront the issue? If your answer is yes, then you're ready. If you're looking forward to confronting them, then you're not ready yet! More than likely, the only reward you'll get from the confrontation is serving your own ego, rather than helping the other person. Your goal should always be to walk in love. Use it as your standard.

Matthew 18:15 (NLT)

"If another believer sins against you, go privately and point out the offense. If the other person listens and confesses it, you have won that person back."

If someone hurts you, the worst place to share it is on social media or at your church's small group. Always start by taking it directly to the person! If that person has done something wrong, you now have a chance to lovingly restore them. If the offense was caused by a misunderstanding, this is the moment where you can both move forward in truth and restoration.

It's a win-win. If, for any reason, the person doesn't receive the correction, all you can do is forgive them and leave it in the Lord's hands.

Treat offense like a hot potato. The longer it stays in your hands, the better chances are that you're going to get burned. The faster you deal with the offense, the less likely it will foster irreconcilable feelings of hurt and bitterness. Learn to let it roll off of you.

I can tell you from first-hand experience, love and forgiveness can become a lifestyle that can leave you free of the burden of offense. Ralph has always had a harder time forgiving people than I have. He used to tell me that it's not fair how easy it is for me to forgive. I could always do it naturally, where Ralph had to "choose" to do it. I can tell you right now, it's not that I'm hurt any less than he is. A long time ago, I *chose* to never let strife dominate my life. I can live in peace, even when someone hurts me, but I know getting overly upset at them is just not worth it.

Galatians 6:1-3 (MSG)

Live creatively, friends. If someone falls into sin, forgivingly restore him, saving your critical comments for yourself. You might be needing forgiveness before the day's out. Stoop down and reach out to those who are oppressed. Share their burdens, and so complete Christ's law. If you think you are too good for that, you are badly deceived.

People don't need to be told their faults. They are probably more aware than anyone else of their shortcomings. What they need is to be loved so they can be restored into the person God created them to be. If we as the church embodied this kind of commitment to restoration, we would at-tract the world in a way we've never seen before. Instead of the church cru-cifying their own when someone messes up, they'd see a family of people encouraging and loving each other through the ups and downs and the messiness of life.

Throwing love at people is like throwing water bombs at a fire. Eventually, with enough bombs, you'll be able to put out any size of fire. Eventually, as you continue to love and forgive others, you'll see love transform their lives.

13

THE HOLY SPIRIT DIFFERENCE

Ralph grew up in a Baptist church and therefore always had a great knowledge of Scripture. He also loved God greatly. However, as an adult, he began to realize that something was missing. He saw that some of his Christian friends seemed to have an "edge" that he didn't have—a peace and a boldness that he couldn't seem to access.

What he started to piece together was that those friends were ones who had had an experience and a relationship with the Holy Spirit. There was clearly something they had that he did not. And he wanted it. The difference in Ralph's life after receiving the gift of the Holy Spirit was tangible and changed how he has lived his life.

I want to end this book by introducing you to the amazing person of the Holy Spirit. There is a lot of mystery around this topic for many people. Some Christians even shy away from the Holy Spirit completely. But He is the key to living a life of power. I would be amiss not to share with you about who He is and how His power can be present in your life.

Who is The Holy Spirit?

The Trinity is made up of God the Father, God the Son (Jesus) and God the Holy Spirit. Each one is equally God, and equally holy. He is not a thing, but a person, just as much as the Father or Jesus. Before Jesus came to earth, all three were in heaven, with the exception of occasional visitations on Earth. Jesus came in a physical form and now sits at the right hand of the Father, in heaven. As much as we talk about Jesus being with us, he is actually in heaven with the Father. Who is with us on earth? The Holy Spirit. He came to us shortly after Jesus went back to be with the Father, on the day of Pentecost. The Bible tells us that Jesus returned to heaven in order for the Holy Spirit to be given to us.

John 7:39
But the Spirit had not yet been given, because Jesus had not yet entered into his glory.

Let's get the revelation that the Holy Spirit is now on earth, and is the only part of God who is here with us! Do you see why it's so important that we meet and know who He is?

What Does He Do?

John 14:26 (AMP)
But the Comforter (Counselor, Helper, Intercessor, Advocate, Strengthener, Standby), the Holy Spirit, Whom the Father will send in My name [in My place, to represent Me and act on My behalf], He will teach you all things. And He will cause you to recall (will remind you of, bring to your remembrance) everything I have told you.

The list of what the Holy Spirit does for us is huge. He's our helper and counselor! In both Ralph's and my life, He has helped us through things in which we had no idea what to do—especially how to start or run a church. But the Holy Spirit did. He counseled us and walked us through it. He helped us put systems and programs in place, that were way beyond our knowledge and experience. He helped us advise people when we had no idea how to find answers. When we were low on strength and power, He was the one who came and operated through us by making us strong!

One of the greatest things the Holy Spirit does is act on behalf of Jesus. He represents Him on earth and in our lives. When we have the Holy Spirit within us, we have the very spirit of Jesus in us! That's why Jesus told us it was so important that He go to be with the Father so that the Holy Spirit could be released on the earth for us. When Jesus was on earth, there was only one of Him. With the Holy Spirit, now available to all of us, it's like millions of little Jesus' operating on the earth!

He also gives us a boldness to share Jesus!

Acts 1:8

But you will receive power when the Holy Spirit comes upon you. And you will be my witnesses, telling people about me everywhere—in Jerusalem, throughout Judea, in Samaria, and to the ends of the earth.

It's the Holy Spirit that makes us effective in our Christian walk, and in our God-given commission to share the good news of Jesus with the world. Most of the great revivals of our time were all birthed through individuals who were Spirit-filled. We also generally don't see people operate in consistent signs and wonders who are not Spirit- filled.   Why? Because without the power and boldness of the Holy Spirit, we will operate in our natural, instead of His supernatural.

Jesus' Baptism

Reading about Jesus' Baptism will explain how the Holy Spirit lives in us.

Luke 3:21-22

When all the people were being baptized, Jesus was baptized too. And as he was praying, heaven was opened and the Holy Spirit descended on him in bodily form like a dove. And a voice came from heaven: "You are my Son, whom I love; with you I am well pleased."

Not only was Jesus baptized in water, but He was also baptized in the Spirit! The interesting thing you'll notice if you keep reading is that it's only after Jesus is baptized that He starts His ministry. In fact, it was immediately after being baptized that Jesus went into the desert for forty days and nights. It was the power of the Holy Spirit on Him that enabled him to endure every temptation that the devil threw at Him.

Notice that the Holy Spirit came on Jesus like a dove. Quite a stark contrast to how the Holy Spirit comes on us today.

Matthew 3:11 (NIV)
"I baptize you with water for repentance. But after me will come one who is more powerful than I, whose sandals I am not fit to carry. He will baptize you with the Holy Spirit and with fire."

The Holy Spirit came on Jesus like a dove and on us as fire. On the day of Pentecost, the Holy Spirit appeared as tongues of fire on each person. Why a dove for Jesus and fire for us? Because Jesus had no sin; He was blameless and pure. You and I have "stuff" that needs to be burned off. Fire burns up garbage! The fire of the Holy Spirit in our lives burns up the garbage of our past. The stuff that gets on us day after day from living in a fallen world. The power of the Holy Spirit burns that off! He allows us to live free and empowered.

I find that when I feel the "yuck" of life on me, all I need to do is pray in the Holy Spirit for awhile. It just seems to burn off! There's a refreshing feeling that comes as the garbage in my life is burned away, and peace returns.

Wasn't I Filled With the Holy Spirit When I Got Saved?
People are often taught that you are filled with the Holy Spirit the moment you are saved. That's not the way the New Testament talks about it.

Acts 19:2
He asked them, "Did you receive the Holy Spirit when you believed?" They answered, "No, we have not even heard that there is a Holy Spirit."

"*. . . when you believed.*" Here Paul is talking to people who had already accepted Jesus. If the Holy Spirit automatically fills believers at the moment of salvation, he would have never had to ask the question! They would have already received Him. But clearly, he is saying here it's a separate experience.

Sealed by the Holy Spirit

There needs to be some clarification on this topic. When we are saved and accept Jesus, we do indeed receive a portion of the Holy Spirit.

> **Ephesians 1:13 (TNIV)**
> *And you also were included in Christ when you heard the word of truth, the gospel of your salvation. Having believed, you were marked in him with a seal, the promised Holy Spirit.*

Here it says that the Holy Spirit marked us with a seal. A seal is something on the outside of a package that protects and identifies an object. A seal is not on the inside; it's merely an exterior mark. At the point of salvation, the Holy Spirit marks you as His. All of heaven and hell can now see that you belong to God.

> **Acts 2:4 (NLT)**
> *And everyone present was filled with the Holy Spirit and began speaking in other languages, as the Holy Spirit gave them this ability.*

On the day of Pentecost, people were not sealed with the Holy Spirit, they were filled. There's a huge difference between an outer seal and an inner filling. A filling of the Holy Spirit permeates every part of you. It changes who you are. An outer seal only identifies and marks you. A seal doesn't change the contents of a package, it only identifies and protects them.

I was filled with the Holy Spirit at the age of nine. I truly felt the power of it in my life, though I didn't fully understand the impact of it at the time since I was just a child. Ralph, on the other hand, had experienced life with and without the power of the Holy Spirit. Though he was saved at five years of age, he was filled with the Spirit at 23.

The best analogy of the difference between the seal of the Spirit on us and the filling of the Spirit is the difference between a blowtorch and a lighter. A lighter does indeed produce a flame, and you can get some basic tasks done with it. If you need to start a fire or light a candle, it will definitely get the job done! But if you need to weld some metal together, it doesn't matter how many hours you stand there with a lighter flickering a flame on that metal. It just won't get the job done! It's not enough power! But take a blowtorch to that metal, the job is done in no time at all.

That's the difference between the Holy Spirit being a seal on us, and Him completely filling us. Even if we have only a portion of Him in our lives, He will still be able to empower us to a limited degree. But when it comes to the tougher issues of life, it's not enough! Hard situations will leave you frustrated if you can't tap into enough power to overcome them. When you need to see the supernatural happen in your life, you need the strength of the Holy Spirit to push through those miracles!

It's a Gift

Being filled with the Holy Spirit is a gift that God wants to give to all of us! It's not a gift that was left for the disciples 2,000 years ago, but a gift that God designed for us all to live with.

Acts 2:39
And you will receive the gift of the Holy Spirit. The promise is for you and your children and for all who are far off—for all whom the Lord our God will call.

We are part of those who are far off that the Lord has called. That means that the gift is for us. There's also another huge benefit to being filled with the Holy Spirit. It's something people often misunderstand: speaking in tongues.

Acts 2:1-4 (NLT)
On the day of Pentecost all the believers were meeting together in one place. Suddenly, there was a sound from heaven like the roaring of

a mighty windstorm, and it filled the house where they were sitting.
Then, what looked like flames or tongues of fire appeared and settled
on each of them. And everyone present was filled with the Holy Spirit
and began speaking in other languages, as the Holy Spirit gave them
this ability.

Everyone was filled and began speaking in other languages, or tongues. This is the evidence that you have been filled with the Holy Spirit. Though not everyone does speak in tongues, I believe everyone who has asked to be filled, can receive the ability. Sometimes our mental reservations just don't let our tongue loosen up enough to be led by the Holy Spirit.

Speaking in tongues is having the Holy Spirit pray for you! How amazing is that? I don't know about you, but sometimes I get stuck in a situation or feel led to pray for someone and have no idea how to pray. During those times I pray in tongues! Who better than the Holy Spirit, who knows the perfect and divine will of God, to have prayed for me and through me!

A few years ago Ralph suddenly felt burdened to pray for me. He didn't know why, or what I needed at that moment, so he started praying in tongues. What he didn't realize was that exactly five minutes after he prayed, there was a near disaster that I was about to have.

I was driving on the interstate in the middle lane with all my boys and my mom when I turned a bend on the highway and saw a huge ladder laying across my lane. I went to slam on my brakes, but looked in my rearview mirror and saw a huge semi-truck right on my tail! Hitting the brakes wasn't an option. There had been solid traffic on both sides of me, and there was no clear way for me to swerve without hitting someone else. I screamed out "Jesus," and immediately saw an opening in the lane to my right. I was able to quickly swerve and avoid disaster. But boy was it close! Ralph praying in the Spirit prayed the very angels of heaven into action to come and protect us. When we don't know how to pray, the Spirit will pray perfectly.

Being Built Up

Praying in tongues, or praying in the Spirit, builds you up. It's like pumping fuel into an empty tank. It helps you go farther and operate in greater spiritual strength. When life drains you, praying in the Spirit refills you!

Jude 1:20

But you, dear friends, build yourselves up in your most holy faith and pray in the Holy Spirit.

There's a direct correlation between speaking in tongues and being strengthened!

1 Corinthians 14:4 (NLT)

A person who speaks in tongues is strengthened personally.

My life changed when I realized that praying in tongues wasn't just the evidence of something that happened to me years ago but something I could use every day to edify myself. Ever since then, I have spoken in tongues every single day. While I drive, shower, or work around the house; whenever I can! It builds me up!

As I pray in the Spirit, I pray the perfect will of God over my life. Since I'm praying forth the right answers ahead of time, it's amazing when I walk into situations how God seems to already have answers lined up for me. He already has wisdom and favor that's gone ahead of me. It's a great way to do life.

How Do I Receive?

Just as we received salvation through faith, we ask God for the gift of the Holy Spirit and, by faith, receive it.

Luke 11:13

So if you sinful people know how to give good gifts to your children, how much more will your heavenly Father give the Holy Spirit to those who ask him.

Your life will never be the same! Some people instantly feel the power of the Holy Spirit on them. For others, it hits them a few days or weeks later. In both cases, always remember that you don't receive it by feelings, you receive it by faith.

My Prayer for You

Thank you for taking this journey with me. My prayer is that God reveals Himself to you and that you receive a revelation through the principles of this book that will bring life-changing victory to you and your family. I encourage you to go deeper into the things I have taught you. Read this book again, break it down chapter by chapter, and take the time to apply the principles. If you want to learn more on how to live victoriously, check out our curriculum. Our Victorious Living DVD set explores many of the topics found in this book but much more in depth!

Ephesians 3:16-20 (NLT)

I pray that from his glorious, unlimited resources he will empower you with inner strength through his Spirit. Then Christ will make his home in your hearts as you trust in him. Your roots will grow down into God's love and keep you strong. And may you have the power to understand, as all God's people should, how wide, how long, how high, and how deep his love is. May you experience the love of Christ, though it is too great to understand fully. Then you will be made complete with all the fullness of life and power that comes from God. Now all glory to God, who is able, through his mighty power at work within us, to accomplish infinitely more than we might ask or think.

■ ■ ■

ACKNOWLEDGEMENTS

First and foremost I am so grateful that God never gave up on me. That He was ever so patient and lovingly guided me through learning and walking out this amazing journey with Him. I owe Him everything.

I am forever grateful to be married to a man who is so secure in himself and the calling God has on his life, that he is not intimidated with a wife who has a strong calling on hers. It was because of Ralph that I stepped into ministry in the first place. It was 2006 and he wanted to stop teaching a men's group, and instead teach a class side by side with me. I was highly resistant! I was great in front of people so long as teaching or preaching were not involved. But he insisted that we work on the content together, and then I would just sit beside him on a stool, making him look good while he delivered the lesson. Well, about 10 minutes into that evening, the Holy Spirit gave me words to speak, and I haven't stopped speaking since! Thank you Ralph for believing in me when I was so far from believing in myself. For being fully persuaded that God is using women in a powerful way in these end days, and for fully encouraging me to run to the ends of the earth if necessary to fulfill the call of God on my life. Thank you for being my biggest cheerleader! I love you.

To my boys for allowing me to understand that one of the greatest ministries of my life has been to raise four powerful men of God. God has such amazing futures for each one of you, and I am humbled daily that God has allowed me to be part of it. I am so proud of you all, and I have loved watching you grow into amazing men of purpose! Each of you has uniquely powerful talents and abilities that God is developing in you to impact the world. To my daughter-in-love, Molly, and beautiful granddaughter Gia; and my future daughter-in-love, Rachael: thank you for bringing me the joy of girls and embracing me so fully in your lives!

You'll never know how much that has meant. God's plans for you go beyond what you could imagine! I love you all!

Thank you to my amazing parents Ted & Rheta Bradford for giving me a spiritual foundation that is second to none. Dad is now in heaven, and how I often long to have him with us in this journey of ministry. I have yet to find a person who has served the church and God's Kingdom as a volunteer as fully as my dad did. He understood honoring authority, and gave everything to the work of God. Mom, in your sincere humility you have no idea how many of thousands of people you have impacted, simply by being who you are. Including me and my family. Without all your help keeping my family and home in order I would never be able to do what I do. Thank you! You are a daily blessing to me.

Thank you to my brother Jim, and friends Tim Storey, and Darryl & Tracy Strawberry. Each one of you has made profound impacts in my life. The fact that you all have believed in me and what God has called me to do humbles me. Thank you for your support, your prayers, your dear friendship and your endorsement of this book.

Thank you to all the friends, family and mentors who have transformed my life with their teaching and with their love and support. Mentors and pastors who invested time one-on-one with me, and those whom I only know from afar but who deeply impacted how I viewed God and His plan for me. I am so grateful that each of you has been faithful to the path God had you walk. I am one who has been impacted through it all.

Of course, I must thank my church family The Source! I still marvel and am completely humbled that such an amazing group of people would dare to call me their Pastor, and willingly do life side by side with me. Thank you! I have some of the most amazing Pastors, leaders, staff and volunteers who surround me and help me do what I do. I could never begin to name them, but you know who you are! You honor me, you serve God with me, and you run with the vision alongside me. Thank you for your undying support and love. This journey of pastoring you has grown me more than anything else in my life, and I truly wouldn't trade a moment of it for anything.

A final thank you to my awesome editors! Stefan Junaeus, thank you for helping me in more ways than I can ever imagine. You brought clarity and structure when I felt overwhelmed, and helped me bring to life the message I knew God wanted me to deliver. You're amazing! And to Pat Mohr who has been an amazing proof editor. Not only have I loved you and your beautiful heart for so many, many years, but you were absolutely a dream to work with! Thank you! May God fully reward you for serving His purposes.

Further Resources

Victorious Living DVD 20 Session Curriculum
(also includes all audio on MP3)
Go deeper with the principles of Victorious Living!

More on Tithing
Book: **Anointed to Prosper by Ralph Hoehne**
This quick-read book will break down the fundamental principles on
tithing with practical teaching and application.

More on Accessing Your Inheritance (2 CD Set)
'Loaves & Fishes Anointing" by Ralph & Joanne Hoehne

More on Iniquities (4 CD Set)
'Why Am I Like This?' by Ralph & Joanne Hoehne

Breaking Through by Joanne Hoehne
(3 CDs or 3 CD/DVD set)
This will help you gain an understanding of how to not only receive
a miracle, but also how to defend it and walk in lifelong breakthrough

Order online at: www.JoanneHoehne.com
or
Call us at: 941-592-4700

ABOUT THE AUTHOR

After great success in the business world, God called Joanne and her husband in late 2007 to step out and plant The Source Church. Ralph and Joanne now co-pastor The Source Church with campuses in Florida and Manitoba, Canada. Their unique side-by-side teaching style each week helps capture the hearts and minds of all ages, with easy to understand analogies and life-applicable principles. They also speak at conferences and seminars, together or individually, bringing practical life-changing messages for people to find and walk in victory.

Joanne strongly believes in men and women both being powerfully used in ministry, and feels called to help pave the way as both a female lead pastor and an equipper of women pastors and leaders both in her own church, as well as women serving across the body of Christ.

In January 2015 Joanne launched a Movement called **SHE** Tour - **S**aved **H**ealed **E**mpowered. A women's conference that has literally brought radical revival to hundreds of women from all walks of life. This conference holds multiple events across North America each year, with a heart to see women become fully alive in all that God has called them to be.

Originally from Winnipeg, Canada, Joanne moved to Florida in 2004 where she now resides with her husband Ralph and four sons Brett, Ashton, Connor and Logan, daughters-in-love Molly & Rachael, and granddaughter Gia. Her favorite things to do are spend time with her family, travel, and enjoy weekly date nights with her husband.

Learn more at www.JoanneHoehne.com or www.ExperienceSHE.com.

Contact us at: 941-592-4700
    Email: info@tapintothesource.com

Follow her on Twitter @joannehoehne